HUMAN RESOURCE
MANAGEMENT

HUMAN RESOURCE
MANAGEMENT

Dr. Veena Christy

Dr. R. Jayanthi

Sandaboina Shivakumar

red'shine

Publication

INDIA

HUMAN RESOURCE MANAGEMENT

by: Dr. Veena Christy, Dr. R. Jayanthi, Sandaboina Shivakumar

■

RED'SHINE PUBLICATION PVT. LTD.

Headquarters (India): 88-90 REDMAC, Navamuvada,

Lunawada, India-389 230

Contact: +91 76988 26988

Registration no. GJ31D0000034

In Association with,

RED'MAC INTERNATIONAL PRESS & MEDIA. INC

India | Sweden | UK

■

■

ISBN: 978-93-93239-99-0

ISBN-10: 93-93239-99-1

DIP: 18.10.9393239991

DOI: 10.25215/9393239991

Price: ₹ 400

April, 2022 (First Edition)

■

■

www.redshine.co.in | info@redshine.in

Printed in India | Title ID: 9393239991

CONTENTS

SR.NO.	MODULE	PAGE NO.
1	**UNIT-1** CONCEPT OF HUMAN RESOURCE MANAGEMENT	1
2	**UNIT-2** PERSPECTIVES IN HUMAN RESOURCE MANAGEMENT	11
3	**UNIT-3** HUMAN RESOURCE PLANNING	25
4	**UNIT-4** CONCEPT OF TRAINING	49
5	**UNIT-5** PERFORMANCE EVALUATION AND CONTROL PROCESS	71
6	**UNIT-6** INDUSTRIAL RELATIONS	88
*	REFERENCES	108

CONCEPT OF HUMAN RESOURCE MANAGEMENT

Human resource management was originally referred as personnel or people management. Since then, it's grown to play a far more significant role. Every business and organisation makes use of formal human resources management. This must be in place in every company and its management.

The personnel department's primary responsibilities include recruiting, evaluating, training, and remuneration. When an employee has a problem at work, the human resources department is there to help. Specifically, Human Resources (HR) is concerned with the impact of specific work practises on an organization's overall success.

Human resources and performance management are intertwined, as seen by the aforementioned criterion. The success of many high-performing firms is increasingly understood to be dependent on their employees' knowledge and abilities, or, human capital. The economic value of employees with the appropriate levels of education, training, and experience is referred to as "human capital." The value of their knowledge and talents can be measured in dollars. For any company to maintain a competitive advantage, human capital management is essential. As a human resource role, it is perhaps the most critical.

DEFINITIONS OF HRM

To begin, HRM is defined as "the systematic and comprehensive management of people in businesses." Traditionally, HRM has been defined as a modernized version of Personnel Management, which some experts see as a precursor to HRM.

"The management of people in organizations from a macro perspective, i.e. managing people in the form of a collective relationship between management and employees."

People enablement and development are key to HR's work in modern firms, and it's all about making the "employment relationship" a positive one that benefits both employers and employees alike.

An organization's HR department is responsible for hiring, motivating, and retaining employees.

"HRM is concerned with the most effective use of people to achieve organizational and individual goals. It is the way of managing people at work, so that they give their best to the organization".

In common language, HRM is "concerned with the people dimension in management. Since every organization is made up of people, acquiring their services, developing their skills, motivating them to high levels of performance and ensuring that they continue to maintain their commitment to the organization are essential for achieving organizational objectives. This is true regardless of the type of organization government business, Education, Health, regression or social action."

"The HRM is the process of attracting, holding and motivating all manager line and staff."

"That part of management which is concerned with people at work and with their relationship within an enterprise. Its aim is to bring together and develop into an effective organization of the men and women who make up an enterprise and having regard for the well-being of the individuals and of working groups, to enable them to make their best contribution to its success."

"The art of recruiting, developing and maintaining qualified workers to meet the objectives of an organization in an efficient and effective manner."

FUNCTIONS OF HUMAN RESOURCE MANAGEMENT

(1) Managerial Functions:

Managing the human resources of an organization is under the purview of the human resources manager. When it comes to his department, he is responsible for directing and coordinating all of its activities.

These functions are briefly discussed below:

I. Planning:

A management must prepare in advance if he or she wants to get things done with the help of employees. Defining the goals of the organization and establishing rules and processes to achieve those goals necessitates planning. Planned personnel programmes for the human resource management are those that will help achieve business objectives such as anticipating vacancies and planning job requirements and descriptions as well as the sources of recruiting.

II. Organising:

Organizational structure must be designed and developed by the human resources management to carry out the various operations once objectives have been set.

The following components make up the organization's basic structure:

Delegation of power according to the tasks assigned and duties involved, as well as the coordination of operations of various employees, are all examples of logical groupings of personnel activity into functions and roles.

III. Directing:

People are responsible for carrying out the plans. People's motivation is a major factor in how easily plans are implemented. As a human resource manager, you are responsible for ensuring that your employees are motivated and committed to the success of the company.

To put it another way, the role of the director is to motivate and guide the employees to complete the company's personnel programmes.

IV. Controlling:

An organization's goals are used to develop its plans, which are then used to regulate its operations according to those plans. Analyzing findings against predetermined benchmarks and making adjustments for any discrepancies is part of the process.

OPERATIVE FUNCTIONS:

1. Procurement of Human Resource / Employment:

The first and most crucial role of HRM is to find and hire the suitable people for the organization's needs. A variety of HRM tasks, such as manpower planning, are required in order to effectively fulfil procurement responsibilities, including estimating the number of people needed.

There are two main types of analysis that are used in a job analysis: a job description that outlines the job's responsibilities as well as a job specification, which specifies what kind of people are needed to do the job.

Then, assigning the most qualified individuals to the positions that need to be filled. Set up an induction programme for the new employee and provide him or her all the knowledge he or she needs in order to build a positive impression of the company.

Development:

A company's training and development of employees follows the hiring process. As a manager, it is your responsibility to ensure that every employee receives the training they need to excel in their current position as well as to prepare them for advancement within the company.

To improve their ability to accomplish their jobs and meet their own personal growth goals, organizations must invest in their employees' education and training needs. Human resources departments will devise training programmes for this aim. There are a variety of training options accessible, both on and off the job.

A well-rounded training programme should incorporate both types of training. Human resources arranges for training not just for new employees, but also for experienced employees to refresh their skills in the application of the latest techniques.

Compensation:

Reimbursement for employees should take into account their fundamental needs, job requirements, legal minimum wage standards and other factors such as an organization's ability to pay, salary levels offered by competitors, etc. The human resources department can use job evaluation and performance evaluation to set salary levels.

Appraisal:

For making significant personnel choices, performance evaluation is the systematic review of each employee's performance and contribution. Training needs and transfer and promotion decisions are made based on the outcomes of performance evaluations. The HR Manager is responsible for designing the appraisal procedures and arranging for managers to be trained in conducting systematic evaluations of their staff.

Motivation:

Employees are motivated to work in the company by the fulfilment of their own desires. A large number of organizations find that their staff isn't doing enough to help them achieve their goals.

Personnel Records:

The company's human resources department is responsible for keeping track of all of the company's employees. It maintains comprehensive records of their education, accomplishments, transfers, and promotions, among other things. Many additional records about employee behaviour, such as absences and turnover, and the organization's personnel programmes and policies are also preserved by this system.

Industrial Relations:

The human resources manager is now also responsible for ensuring good workplace relations. They can assist in collective bargaining, conciliation, and conflict resolution in the event that they are required to do so. This is due to the fact that he has access to all personnel information and is familiar with numerous labour laws.

Keeping the peace in the workplace can be done a great deal by a company's human resources management, as he or she is involved in numerous committees dealing with discipline, labour welfare, safety, and grievances. Employees' grievances can be addressed through the establishment of a grievance procedure. In addition, he serves as a conduit for the ideas of labour leaders to the company's upper management by providing them with accurate information.

Separation: Human resource management's first task is to find and hire personnel, thus it makes sense that the final step is to let them go and restore them to their previous roles in society. There are very few persons that die while at work.

HUMAN RESOURCES DEVELOPMENT (HRD) – DEFINITION

Human resource development is the process of preparing more skilled and competent individuals to meet the organization's current and future needs. Human resource development benefits both the employee and the organisation. It benefits people by expanding their skill set, while also benefiting businesses by attracting more competent individuals.

GOALS OF HRD
Resource planning

It is critical for any firm to have the proper person for the job at the right time. Resource planning is the procedure through which this is ensured.

Recruitment and selection

Recruiting and selection processes are in place to guarantee that we hire people with the proper skills and attitudes. To be sure, there is no such thing as a correct or incorrect attitude in general. By the correct attitude, we mean one that is compatible with the company's work culture.

Training and development

This is done in order to retain personnel while also improving their skill set, which benefits both the firm and the employee. A well-trained workforce equates to increased production, which results in increased profit.

Performance appraisal

This is a process of feedback. Employees' performance is reviewed on a variety of parameters, and they receive feedback as well as suggestions for improvement. If an employee's performance does not improve over time, the organisation may terminate him or her.

Remuneration

This is a procedure for determining whether employees are being compensated fairly. By "well compensated," we imply that they receive a salary and wages commensurate with industry standards. Additionally, this method verifies whether the granted amount is justified by the employee's performance. If the performance is above average, more perks may be awarded; nevertheless, if the performance is below average, certain deductions may be made.

Motivation

Motivation is another critical aspect in human resource management. We frequently lose track of time and require external encouragement. This is the procedure that ensures the external push is delivered on time and in the correct manner.

Overall well being of the workforce

Human resource development strives to ensure the employee's physical and emotional well-being. Additionally, it aims to improve employees' social lives by increasing their possibilities for engagement and interaction in internal, external, formal, or informal organisations. A physically fit and intellectually strong individual, equipped with the necessary skills and mindset, is an extremely valuable asset to any firm.

CHALLENGES OF HUMAN RESOURCE DEVELOPMENT

Changing Workforce Demographics

Demographic trends have already had a significant impact on human resource departments worldwide. The labour force has become increasingly diversified, compelling organisations to fundamentally alter their approach to human resource management in order to keep pace with market realities.

Eliminating Skills Gap

We had already addressed how businesses must hire educated workers in order to compete successfully in a global economy.

HRM SUPPORT FOR IMPROVEMENT PROGRAMS
Improve your hiring process

If you want to run a scalable business, you must first develop a strong team of experienced individuals that are prepared to stay with the company for an extended period of time. Individuals who are well acquainted will be more driven and thus more productive. To establish a staff of this calibre, you'll need to invest time in pre-employment screening and learning as much as possible about a prospective employee. Verify their criminal history and any improperly supplied information. Ascertain as much information as possible about their requirements, expectations, habits, and motivation. Once you've gathered all of this information compare the results and construct a team that is cohesive and prepared to grow.

Work on reward programs

Punishment is one method of motivating individuals; a much more effective method is to reward them. To keep your employees happy and engaged, you must recognise their accomplishments. Your first priority should be their health. Individuals that are recognised for their efforts are more productive and will gladly spend eight hours a day working for you.

Utilize HR software

Human resource software is specifically intended for small and medium-sized enterprises and will turn human resource administration from a time-consuming, hard procedure involving spreadsheets or out-of-date software into a quick, easy, and simple one. Utilizing this programme will save you a significant amount of time and money, allowing you to reallocate funds elsewhere.

WORK LIFE BALANCE

Work-life balance has long been a concern for individuals concerned with the quality of work and its relationship to overall life quality. The impact of child labour was a key worry throughout the early stages of the industrial revolution in Europe (and continues to be in some parts of the developing world today). Yet work-life balance has risen to prominence in current debates, largely because excessive work demands are viewed as a distinct issue that must be handled in rich nations.

WORK-LIFE BALANCE – DEFINITIONS

Nowadays, the concept of Work-Life Balance is not novel; it has been thoroughly debated due to its critical nature. It has been defined as an individual's orientation toward numerous life roles and the phenomenon of interroles. Different researchers have expressed varying perspectives on the topic of work-life balance. Several critical definitions include the following:

living a balanced life as "achieving gratifying experiences in all life domains, which demands a well-balanced distribution of personal resources such as energy, time, and commitment across domains." work-family balance as "happiness and optimal performance at work and at home with the least amount of role conflict possible." balance as "a fulfilling, healthy, and productive life that incorporates work, play, and love."

SIGNIFICANCE OF WORK-LIFE BALANCE

Work-Life Balance is becoming increasingly crucial as people struggle with decreasing workplaces and increased time constraints. Work-life initiatives benefit both employees and businesses, as they raise productivity, employee well-being, save expenses, improve retention and recruiting, and boost staff motivation and morale. According to many ideas, work-life balance policies aim to reduce stress and contribute to a healthier and safer work environment. Employees want their employers to understand that they have a life outside the job that includes family, friends, and social gatherings. According to studies, an unbalanced workforce experiences stress and discontent, resulting in decreased family and work engagement. Work-life balance difficulties are a leading cause of workers quitting their jobs. Thus, work-life balance is a critical and growingly popular topic since it strives to improve people's quality of life while also boosting access to job possibilities and paid employment. Larger businesses are more likely to provide extended and paid parental leave as well as flexible work hours.

●

PERSPECTIVES IN HUMAN RESOURCE MANAGEMENT

EVOLUTION OF HUMAN RESOURCE MANAGEMENT

In comparison to other countries, HR management in India is a relatively new phenomenon. Arthasastra" by Kautilya, which was written in 400 B.C., deals with certain fundamental issues of human resources management. Kautilya's HRM approaches were used by the government in those days. It has only evolved in its modern form since the country gained its independence. However, it wasn't until 1948 that the appointment of labour and welfare officers really took off, despite their relevance being recognised as early as 1929. Section 49 of the Act mandated that enterprises with more than 500 employees have Welfare Officers. Only a few aspects of workers' wellbeing were initially addressed by the government.

RECENT DEVELOPMENTS:

Human resources management has recently evolved to regard employees as economic, social, psychological, and spiritual individuals. Annually, we've outlined some of the most notable developments in human resources management.

- In 1995, the focus on human resources development was switched (HRD).
- In 1998, HRD, cultural diversity, teamwork, and participatory management remained a focal point of corporate strategy. Emerging trends include complete quality and employee empowerment, the development of empowered teams and HRM being integrated into strategy, as the top management realises that human resources are essential to 21st century organizations.

- National Commission on Labor was established for this purpose in the year 1999.
- Sizing organizations in an efficient manner has been a major focus in this year.
- Attitude is now more important than skill and knowledge when it comes to finding a new job or employee in 2002.
- Change from a hierarchical structure to one that is more flexible and virtual occurred in 2005.

In 2006, human resources management (HRM) became the foundation of strategic management.

Human resource management has been reduced to the status of "human capital management" in the year 2007.

Due to the ongoing global economic and crisis, employment losses, pay costs, and layoffs continued in 2009.

HUMAN FACTOR

"Human factors" are defined as "environmental, organisational, and job elements, as well as human and individual traits, that influence workplace behaviour in ways that can affect health and safety."

IMPORTANCE OF THE HUMAN FACTOR

"Human factors are critical because they contribute to the efficiency, effectiveness, and safety of work. Human-factors-aware organisations will guarantee that machines and equipment are simple and safe to operate for their employees.

• Appropriate use of additional resources
- Contribute to the transformation of inanimate factors of production into usable products

CHALLENGES IN HRM
Managing the Vision:

The organization's vision guides corporate strategy and assists managers in evaluating management processes and making decisions. As a result, vision management will become an intrinsic part of the process of human resource management in the future.

Internal Environment

Creating an environment that is responsive to external changes, satisfying people, and capable of being sustained through culture and processes is a difficult undertaking.

AFFIRMATIVE ACTION

It is a programme or policy of a business that strives to eliminate discrimination through equal opportunity and professional advancement.

Affirmative action programmes take into account variables such as "race, colour, religion, sexual orientation, or national origin" in order to assist an underrepresented group, typically as a means of mitigating the impacts of a history of discrimination.

Affirmative action
Attract a diverse workforce
Purpose

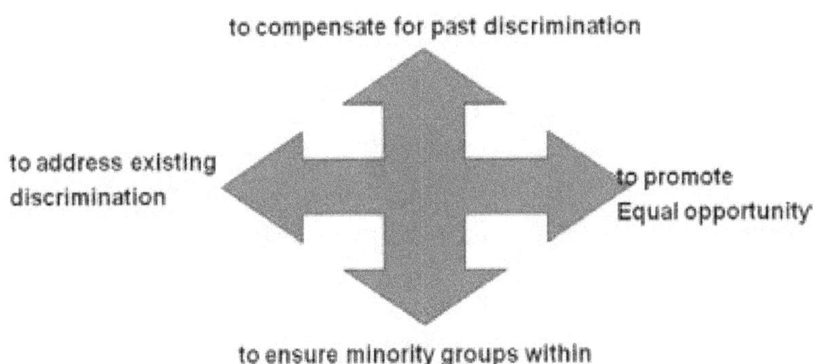

INCLUSIVE GROWTH

The inclusive growth method is more long-term in nature, as it places a premium on productive employment.

Examples

There will be an increase in the number of productive jobs produced.

Economic opportunity has been broadened for everyone.

Income redistribution on a direct basis

Increasing the wages of marginalised groups

ROLE OF HUMAN RESOURCE MANAGEMENT (HRM)

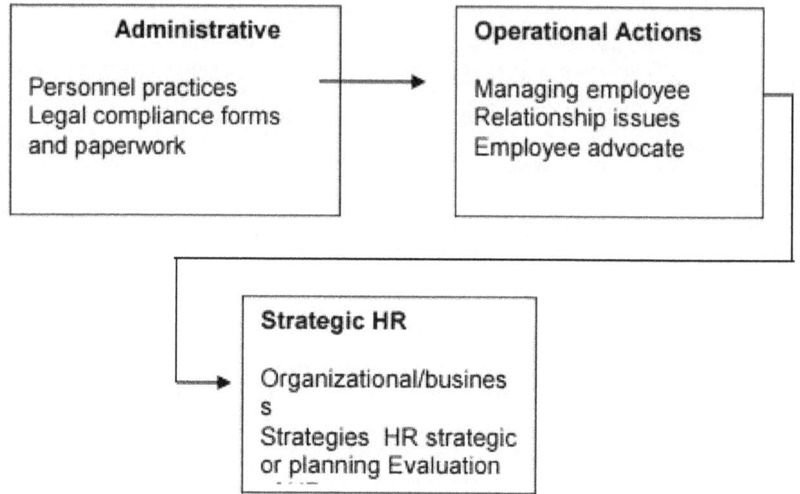

1. Administrative Role of HR

Human resource management's administrative role has historically been primarily weighted toward administration and recordkeeping, which includes required legal paperwork and policy implementation.

2. Operational and Employee Advocate Role for HR

Human resource managers oversee the majority of human resource activities in accordance with management-identified strategy and operations and serve as the employee advocate for employee issues and concerns.

Occasionally, the HR advocate job may cause friction with operations management. Employers, on the other hand, may risk even more litigation and regulatory complaints without the HR advocate role.

3. Strategic Role for HR

Historically, the administrative position has been the major role for human resources. However, as seen in Figure 1.4, a broader transformation of human resources is required such that much less HR time and fewer HR staff members are dedicated to clerical labour.

Despite the fact that this strategic role of human resources is recognised, many businesses have made little headway toward achieving it. The following are some examples of areas where human resources can make a strategic contribution:

Leading efforts to locate new facilities or to relocate operations to overseas outsourcing destinations depending on manpower requirements

Using human resource management technologies to decrease administrative time, equipment, and staff

It is an era where, in order for a firm to succeed competitively, it is necessary to integrate HRM considerably, which necessitates such competencies from human resource specialists.

HUMAN RESOURCE POLICIES

A company's HR policies are the official rules and procedures that it uses to hire new employees, train them, evaluate them, and compensate them. In order to avoid misunderstandings between employees and employers, these regulations should be organised and presented in an easy-to-understand format.

Human resources departments use "best practises," which refers to the manner in which an employment action is handled by specialists in the field. For example, a best practise in human resources.

HR Policies – Need

For instance, in order to terminate an employee in line with applicable employment law requirements, among other things, it is typically essential to adhere to stipulations contained in employment contracts and collective bargaining agreements. The formation of an HR Policy outlining obligations, behaviour standards, and documented disciplinary procedures has become the accepted method for achieving these commitments.

They establish foundations for making consistent decisions and promote equity in how people are treated. Additionally, human resource policies can be quite helpful at sustaining and fostering the ideal company culture.

TYPES OF HR POLICIES

1. Originated Policies

These are purposefully established by top management with the goal of directing executive deliberation at various levels.

2. Appealed Policies –

These policies are designed to address the unique requirements of certain exceptional situations that were not covered by the preceding policies. Typically, such demands come from subordinates who are unable to manage problems according to the direction provided by existing policies.

3. Imposed Policies –

As implied by the names of these policies, they are imposed or compelled by external authorities such as the government, trade associations, and unions.

4. General Policies –

These policies reflect the top management's ideas and priorities in establishing the overarching plan for charting the organization's growth trajectory.

5. Specific Policies –

As implied by their names, these policies address specific issues like as recruiting, remuneration, and collective bargaining. However, such policies should be consistent with the broad framework established by general policies.

6. Written Policies and Implied Policies –

Implied policies are those that are visible in members' behaviour, such as dress code, a pleasant tone when engaging with customers, and not getting angry at work. On the other side, written policies formalize administrative thinking and provide minimal space for interpretation.

COMPUTER APPLICATIONS IN HUMAN RESOURCE MANAGEMENT

Today, information is advancing at a breakneck pace. There is a knowledge explosion taking place. Current knowledge is critical for making sound decisions.

Computers are distinguished by their speed and accuracy. The machine is neither bored nor exhausted. It is capable of handling any volume of data. Computers' speed and accuracy have resulted in swift transactions and other corporate activities. Management receives information more rapidly. The computer offers the management with a big and sophisticated database that may be used at the proper moment to make decisions.

Computer use in HRM:
Human Resource Planning:

Human resource planning requires a large amount of data. Top management wishes to develop a long-term human resource strategy plan. The human resource information system collects the data necessary to make critical estimates about human resource requirements. Additionally, the information can be used to acquire human resources, promote, transfer, and develop career paths.

Training and Development:

Under computer-assisted instruction, the computer assesses the students' ability prior to the commencement of the programme. The assessment process continues throughout the session. The assessment forces the trainer to adapt the training materials to the trainee's specific needs.

As this is a program-based training, there are no charges associated with the trainer. CBT has been enhanced by the incorporation of video, a high-tech training technique known as interactive video training. Additionally, CD-ROMs are employed for executive development. The organisation must determine the most appropriate computerised training technique based on its financial resources and the sort of employees and executives getting training.

There is a continuing need to refresh employees' and executives' skills and knowledge in order to fulfil the organization's rising needs. Computerized training programmes meet these organisational requirements.

Career and Succession Planning:

An in-depth analysis of one's preferences, abilities, skills and competency as well as their alignment with the needs of the company or another organisation at a higher level is what career planning is all about. Each individual, executive, and organisation may rely on the computer to complete this task quickly and accurately.

The organisation has the ability to keep tabs on employees and leaders with lofty goals. These people have a great deal of regard for what they do for a living and how they get there. People in this group aren't afraid to leave an organisation if they don't see progress in their career.

Compensation:

Numerous software programmes are available to manage and monitor compensation administration in this manner. Each month, the employee receives information on his or her salary and mandatory deductions from it, as well as his or her leave records to date.

Performance Appraisal:

When an individual's quality or performance is judged by someone who is superior in rank and hierarchy, there is the possibility of a prejudiced attitude. Computers are capable of providing an unbiased solution to a problem. Modules are offered to assist with performance evaluation. These programmes have multiple grading scales for critical performance categories. By adjusting the rating scale offered by the programme, the organisation can utilise the appropriate scales to evaluate the performance of its personnel of various grades and levels.

Safety and Health:

Safety and health at work are critical. Employees who are disease-free and have all of their body parts intact and secure are the organization's assets. The organisation that possesses such human resources should be proud of themselves. It deserves praise for its outstanding provisions for the safety and health of its personnel.

Employees can be made aware of all of these and warned of the potentially hazardous consequences via computer network at regular intervals or regularly. In this regard, computers can provide the safest and healthiest system for the organization's human resources. Computers assist in preserving health, coping with stress, changing one's lifestyle and adopting the one that is most beneficial to one's health, dieting, and so on.

Human Relations:

Many organisations struggle with improving their human relations. Every organisation desires improved human interactions and smooth operation. The union's connections with management should be cordial and cooperative. Computers can assist in maintaining records of union-management negotiations and the agreements made between the two.

In modern times, multinational corporations are establishing global networks that employ thousands of employees and other officials on a global scale.

HUMAN RESOURCE ACCOUNTING

Human resource accounting can be defined as an accounting system that views human resources as an asset and records all financial expenses associated with human resources, such as wages, compensation, and training, in the books of account. Human resources, like other tangible goods, are valued in accounting books. Assessment, planning, and reporting on human resource costs assist an organisation in effectively tracking its assets and are thus a significant financial component of any business association. Any organization's financial report is entirely dependent on the cost of labour employed.

DEFINITION OF HUMAN RESOURCE ACCOUNTING

"Human resource accounting aims to identify and report on investments in an organization's human capital that are currently unaccounted for in standard accounting practises."

"Human resource accounting is the act of identifying and quantifying human resource data and presenting this data to interested parties."

"Human resource accounting is the process of quantifying and qualifying human organisational inputs such as training experience, request, and commitment."

Human resource accounting is the accounting and acknowledgment of expenses incurred by an organization's personnel. This includes costs associated with recruitment, selection, training, and hiring.

IMPORTANCE OF HUMAN RESOURCE ACCOUNTING

1. Sign of Good Health of the Organisation -

HRA serves as a barometer of an organization's health. The amount of investment made in an organization's human resources assists in estimating the amount of profit that may be realised in the future.

2. Help in Determining the Need of Recruitment -

HRA reports on the changes in the rate of return and the amount of spending that should be made on the organization's manpower. If profits are high, the need for new personnel increases, and if profits are low, no further recruitment occurs. These determinations are made entirely on the basis of information provided by HRA.

3. Facilitates Scheduling and Implementing HR Policies -

An organization's human resource policies encompass policies governing human resource functions such as promotion, training, demotion, and transfer. Appropriate scheduling and implementation of these principles are critical for an organization's seamless operation. This function is managed by an organization's human resource accounting system.

4. Motivates Employees -

Employees become motivated to develop themselves once they learn their true worth in the perspective of the organization's human resource accounting system. The amount invested in them will motivate them to enhance output in proportion to the organization's investment in them.

HUMAN RESOURCES AUDIT

Every organisation need a method for monitoring the varied activities and consequences of the numerous persons that work there. This operation is carried out via the audit process. An audit is a process by which the financial records of any department are systematically examined and validated, which the finance department performs on a regular basis. However, in the context of the human resources department, it can be characterised as an ongoing process of evaluating the effectiveness of all human resource policies, processes, and activities carried out by the organization's employees. It is not simply a technique of recording financial transactions, but also a planning tool. The organisation performs a variety of activities, including recruitment, deployment, training, development, promotion, and retaining talented workers. Human resource auditing aides in the improvement of these functions by finding accessible opportunities for an organisation to capitalise on and become more successful. HR audits also function as a development tool, enhancing not only the performance of its human assets, but also the organisation as a whole.

DEFINITION OF HUMAN RESOURCES AUDIT

"An HR audit examines an organization's human resource activities to determine their effectiveness and efficiency."

"Human resource auditing is concerned with acquiring and evaluating data in order to determine what actions should be made to improve performance."

IMPORTANCE OF HUMAN RESOURCE AUDIT

1) Promoting Critical Business Plans :

Each organisation pursues a set of strategic plans in order to accomplish its objectives. The path to achieving these objectives gets easier if employees share their perspectives on these plans and actively participate in their accomplishment.

2) Role Clarity of HR Functions:

Personnel in the human resources department must be very clear about their duties and responsibilities within the organisation. They should recognise that their first concern should be the organization's interests. Human resource audits perform this role transparency purpose. HR audits not only raise employee knowledge of their responsibility in human resource development, but also direct senior management to assist in HRD efforts.

3) Improving Organisational Competency:

Another advantage of human resource audits is that they aid in determining an organization's competency level. This is accomplished by attempting to ascertain both the strengths and weaknesses of the current administrative structure. If a flaw in the system's operation is discovered, HR audit seeks to propose strategies for increasing productivity. Enhancing employees' strengths and eliminating their flaws has a favourable effect on their performance. These beneficial effects can also be seen in HRIS, work practises, delegation and clarity of roles and duties, and information exchange, among other areas. This, in turn, will contribute to the organization's competency level improvement.

4) Analysis of HR Functions:

HR audit is critical in examining the HR department's operation. It provides an opportunity for the human resources department to compete in a variety of events and prepare for future opponents. Additionally, it serves as a guide for the human resources department's environmental, policy, and training processes. Promotion, maintenance, and counselling, among other things. It aids in analysing employee performance and enhancing their leadership abilities. If necessary, human resource audits assist in re-designing the human resource department's development system.

5) ROI Analysis:

Every organisation spends significant sums on human resource development in the form of recruitment, training programmes, remuneration, and enhancing working conditions, among other things, in order to maximise their Return on Investment (ROI). Thus, human resource audits determine return on investment. Additionally, it assesses the requirement for various training courses and the most effective way to employ them for both human resource development and the corporation's growth. Making these programmes cost effective also helps management become more adept at performing these duties.

6) Increased Focus on Human Resourced Capabilities:

Human resource auditing is a process that focuses on the employees' knowledge, experience, conduct, and outlook. The competencies of personnel at various levels of the organisation (managerial, technical, and human) are identified and appraised. If a discrepancy is discovered between the skills possessed by individuals and those required by the organisation, appropriate measures can be made to close the discrepancy. This can be accomplished through the use of performance appraisals, role clarification exercises, and the like.

7) Strengthening Performance Improvement Mechanisms:

Human resource audits may involve performance development approaches in order to increase employee input. The strategies may include performance management, sharing aspirations with employees, documenting the duties assigned to them, assigning them responsibilities, providing them with a conducive work atmosphere, and so on.

●

HUMAN RESOURCE PLANNING

INTRODUCTION

A company's most critical managerial task is the development of its human resources. For example, it assures appropriate supply of human resources, proper human resource quality, and efficient exploitation of human resource.

Planning for human resources begins with HRP, or Human Resource Planning. Recruiting, on boarding, development, compensation, and evaluation all have their roots in the HRP. There is a wide range of industries and enterprises that benefit from HR planning. Organizational success is directly related to how organisations recruit, select and retain personnel, and HR planning has a direct impact on this process. In light of recent economic changes, HR workforce planning has become even more critical

A company's definition of human resources planning might vary widely. Developing managers is a component of human resources planning for some businesses. The goal of HRP is to make the manager more capable of dealing with the existing and future challenges of the business world.

OBJECTIVES OF HUMAN RESOURCE PLANNING

- Determine the amount of manpower that is needed in the future and devise a recruitment and selection strategy.
- Determining the company's future talent needs.
- Training and development needs of the organization must be determined.
- Avoiding unwarranted detentions or dismissals due to staff shortages or surpluses.

- Keeping a close eye on wages and salaries.
- Accommodating technology advancement and modernization in an organization.
- Making succession plans and ensuring that all employees' career paths are well defined.
- Increasing the efficiency of the workforce

NEED FOR HUMAN RESOURCE PLANNING

1. **Replacement of Persons**: Because to retirement, old age, death, etc., a considerable number of employees must be replaced. In the event of a crisis, people will need to be prepared to assume new roles.

2. **Labour Turnover:** Every company has a constant churn of employees. Although the level of employee turnover varies from company to company, it cannot be completely eradicated. In order to replace individuals who have stepped down, the company will need to find new employees.

3. **Expansion Plans:** In order to expand or diversify a company there will be an increase in the number of new employees needed. Planning for human resources is critical in these kinds of circumstances.

4. **Technological Changes**: The company is operating in a constantly evolving technical landscape. Possibly, new training is required for employees. In addition, there may be a need to bring in new employees. In order to satisfy the increased expectations of the firm, human resource planning is necessary.

5. **Assessing Needs:** Human resource planning is also necessary to identify if the organization has a surplus or a deficit of personnel. The work will suffer if there are fewer people than necessary. As an alternative, if there are more employees than necessary, the cost of labour will rise, and so on. HR planning guarantees that an adequate number of people are employed.

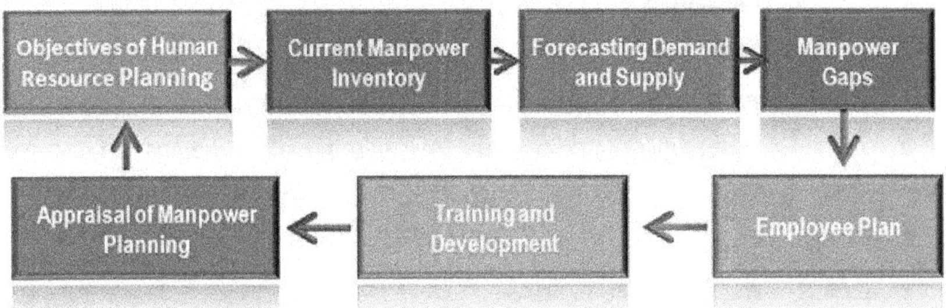

Determining the Objectives of Human Resource Planning:

The first stage in any process is to determine why it is being carried out in the first place. In order to select the right amount of people for the right kind of job, it's critical that the aim of manpower planning be made clear up front.

Marketing, finance, production and human resources may all have different staffing needs based on their respective roles or responsibilities within an organization's many departments.

Analyzing Current Manpower Inventory:

This information can be used to prepare for future staffing needs, including both internal (current employees) as well as external ("outside") recruitment. This means that a steady supply of qualified candidates must be kept on hand in case any positions become available in the near future.

Forecasting Demand and Supply of Human Resources:

Once an inventory of gifted manpower is kept, the next stage is to match the future demand for manpower with the organization's supply or accessible resources.

Analyzing the Manpower Gaps:

After projecting demand and supply, it is simple to determine personnel gaps. If demand exceeds availability of human resources, there is a shortage, and hence additional candidates must be hired.

Employment Plan/Action Plan:

An action plan should be prepared after considering the lack of manpower. There are two options for dealing with a shortfall or surplus in the company's finances: recruiting and training new employees, as well as redeployment and layoffs.

Training and Development:

Existing employees who are obliged to keep their skills current are also given training opportunities.

Appraisal of Manpower Planning:

Finally, the efficacy of the workforce planning process must be examined. Human resource plans are compared to their implementation to ensure that a sufficient number of workers are available in a wide range of positions.

DEMAND FORECASTING:

It is the process of estimating the future requirements for all types and levels of human resources within an organisation.

Methods of Demand Forecasting:
(1) Executive Judgment:

Occasionally, representatives of high management convene and determine needs with the assistance of the personnel department. Forecasts developed in this manner were given to department heads for assessment and, with their permission, the need was authorised. This is referred described as a 'top-down' method. The optimal technique is a hybrid of the two. Executives at both levels, armed with rules, convene to determine the organization's human resource requirements.

(2) Work Load Forecasting:

This technique is often referred to as the work study technique. Each employee's working capacity is expressed in terms of man-hours. The number of man-hours necessary for each unit is determined, followed by the number of required staff.

(3) Statistical Techniques:

Statistical and mathematical methodologies are more responsive to long-range demand forecasts for human resources. Computers provide quick analysis of any type of data.

The following are the forecasting techniques that are utilised in this category:

Econometric Models:

Econometric models are developed using historical statistical data analysis to establish the link between variables in a mathematical formula. The variables are those that determine human resource requirements, such as production, sales, finance, and other operations. Forecasting human resource requirements using an econometric model is dependent on a variety of variables.

Regression Analysis:

Regression analysis is used to estimate future demand for human resources based on factors like as sales, production services given, and so on. When the independent and dependent variables are functionally connected to one another, this method is applied. Computers are now utilised to solve regression equations for the purpose of forecasting demand.

SUPPLY FORECASTING:

Supply forecasting is the process of estimating the supply of human resources by analysing the present inventory of human resources and their future availability.

Sources of Supply:
Internal Factors:

Internal sources of human resources include the product of established employee training programmes and management development programmes for executives, as well as the organization's existing reservoirs of talents, potentials, and creative powers.

External Factors:

External factors might be classified as local or national.

(a) Local Factors:

(1)   Population densities within the enterprise's reach.
(2)   Other employers' current and prospective wage and salary structures.
(3)   Unemployment rate in the local area.
(4)   Employees who are available on a part-time, temporary, or casual basis.
(5)   The product of locally controlled educational and training institutions, both public and private.
(6)   Infrastructure for local transportation and communication.
(7)   Residential facility availability.

(b) National Factors:

National factors include the following:
(1)   Trends in the country's labour force growth.
(2)   Academic, technological, and professional institutions' output.
(3)   The effect of shifting educational trends.
(4)   Patterns of migration and immigration.
(5)   The effect of national educational institutions.

SKILLS INVENTORY

A skills inventory is a company-wide resource that the human resources department utilises. It is a database that records and tracks an organization's personnel' competencies and experience. It is often a thorough and ever-changing list of abilities, education, experiences, and capabilities. Depending on the business, the abilities of your employees may contain a mix of technical and soft talents. While all of these abilities are beneficial to the workforce, skills inventories can assist human resource professionals in identifying skills gaps within the organisation. This establishes a framework for developing training and determining the type of personnel to recruit during the following employment cycle.

SUCCESSION PLANNING

Another application of skills inventories in human resource management is succession planning. Succession planning is a human resource approach that evaluates whether employees may be eligible for promotion if a position becomes available. Utilizing a skills inventory for this purpose equips the human resources department with the confidence and data necessary to fill roles internally when appropriate. Consider a sales lead that performs exceedingly well and has earned the requisite skills to advance to a sales manager role. The human resources department may keep an eye out for this individual in the event that a sales management position becomes available.

Succession planning is a critical activity that focuses on planning and managing an individual's career in order to meet their requirements and aspirations optimally.

JOB ANALYSIS
Meaning and Definition

Analyzing employment in this way is a methodical and in-depth process. For a job, it's a way to figure out exactly what the work entails and who should be employed for it.

Analysis of work duties and nature, as well as who should be employed, is done through a process called job analysis. Examining employment in a systematic manner is called job analysis. It is a methodical investigation of the tasks, responsibilities, and duties that are required to do a job.

The process of analysing, examining, and compiling information about the various parts and functions of a work is known as "job analysis. To put it another way, it's the process of analysing and gathering information on the job's operations and duties. This "job analysis" entails "systematically discovering and recording details about each work" in the words of Yoder.

As a result, conducting a job analysis entails gathering data on the position.

The job analysis may include these activities:

- When looking for a new employee, it's a good idea to have a look at current employees' duties, conduct Internet research, and look at examples of job descriptions online or offline that highlight similar positions.

- In conducting a job analysis, it's critical to have both a clear description of the position and detailed requirements. As a result, the business and its employees are better able to deal with a wide range of issues.

USES OF JOB ANALYSIS

(i)   It aids in anticipating the organization's human resource requirements.

(ii) Job analysis shall include information on the personal characteristics required to perform job-related behaviours for recruiting reasons.

(iii) It serves as the basis for employment evaluations.

(iv) It gives required information to management regarding staff training and development programmes.

(v)   It aids in the establishment of precise standards for the development of the organization's performance appraisal system.

(vi) It enables management to examine the hazards associated with the machinery and tools that must be handled, as well as the work environment, objectively.

(vii) It assists in developing occupations to better fit the employees' mental makeup.

METHODS OF JOB ANALYSIS

Questionnaire:

This is a frequently used technique for gathering job-related data. The questionnaire is organised in such a way that it is possible to collect data on job nomenclature, job descriptions, machines and equipment used, and working circumstances, among other things.

Employees/subordinates and managers complete the questionnaire. The questionnaire should be extremely straightforward, understandable, and pertinent. If the questionnaire does not elicit responses from employees/managers, it should be destroyed and a new one created.

Written Narratives:

The employee maintains a daily log of significant duties accomplished, noting the start and completion times of each activity. This serves as the foundation for narratives, which serve as a vehicle for obtaining information about various vocations. They may be insufficient and disorganised, necessitating the addition of interviews and other sources.

Observations:

The job analyst observes the job while it is being performed in this technique. He verifies the tasks completed on the job, the rate of work, the working environment, and the workplace dangers associated in any given work cycle. He does a job analysis based on these observations. This approach has one significant drawback. It is that the analyst must exercise extreme caution in determining which data to observe and which to disregard. Additionally, he should be able to analyse following observation.

Interviews:

In this strategy, the analyst conducts personal interviews with employees while they are on the job. The data obtained from various employees is entered into a uniform format. The analyst will inquire about normal job-related matters. These interviews are frequently combined with observation tools to elucidate all issues pertaining to the employment under analysis. While employees may not always provide accurate information about their jobs during this research, an intelligent analyst has the capacity to distinguish relevant from irrelevant information.

JOB DESCRIPTION

A job description is a document that outlines the essentials of a position in order to attract the best candidates. As part of an application, potential employees are required to provide a resume and cover letter that includes information such as the position they're applying for; the company they'll be working for; the reporting structure; and the type of the work they'll be doing.

PURPOSE OF JOB DESCRIPTION

- For recruitment personnel, it provides them with a clear picture of what kind of individual is needed in order to do a specific activity or job.
- Aside from that, it lays out exactly who will be reporting to whom.

JOB SPECIFICATION

Additionally, job requirements are also known as employee specifications and are written statements of educational credentials and specific traits and levels of experience required to accomplish a job as well as the responsibilities and other special sensory demands. Everything from general health to IQ to memory to leadership abilities to emotional adaptability to morality to creativity is included in a person's overall well-being.

RECRUITMENT

Recruitment refers to the process of finding and developing new employees and workers for an organization at the time they are needed. Finding, maintaining and contacting the sources of manpower are all part of this process. "Recruitment is the process of searching for prospective employees and stimulating and encouraging them to apply for jobs in the organization."

"Recruitment is a process to discover the sources of manpower to meet the requirement of the staffing schedule and to employ effective measures for attracting that manpower in adequate numbers to facilitate effective selection of an efficient working force."

SOURCES OF RECRUITMENT

Internal Sources: An internal recruitment is one that occurs within the company or organization. When it comes to recruiting, a business has a wealth of options at its disposal. Transfers, promotions, and rehiring of ex-employees are the three most common internal sources.

Employee productivity may rise as a result of an increase in employee motivation as a result of internal recruitment. It also saves money and time. It's also a negative that internal hiring doesn't bring in new talent. Some of the company's workforce needs can't be satisfied through internal hiring. It is necessary to bring in outside help.

Internal sources: 1. Present Employee: An organization's current employees are the most typical source of internal recruitment. When an organization is looking for personnel, it typically keeps an inventory of their qualifications. Job postings are the most common approach for establishing a pool of internal candidates. A person's skills, hobbies, and professional goals are taken into consideration while assessing job prospects internal sources of recruitment include promotions and transfers from within an organization.

2. **Employees Referrals**: As a result, it serves as a good source of internal talent. Employees help their families and friends get a leg up on the competition by informing them about the benefits of a job with the company and even urging them to apply.

This source is a cost-effective method of recruiting because it reaches a large number of qualified candidates at a cheap cost. A key drawback of employee referrals is that the individuals referred are likely to be similar to those already employed by the company.

3. **Former Employees:** Another internal source of recruitment is former employees. Some ex-employees may be willing to return to the workforce on a part-time basis or propose someone who would be a good fit for the organization. People who have left a company for some reason or another may come back and work for the organization from time to time. A benefit of using this source is that you already know how well these folks will perform.

Merits of Internal Recruitment:
a)   It boosts morale and productivity in the workplace.
b)   A sense of security is created among employees as a result.
c)   Employees are aware that they have the opportunity to rise through the ranks. In order to establish their worth, they labour harder.
d)   Internal hiring promotes continuity of employment and stability of the organisation.
e)   The prospect of moving to a new position motivates employees to keep learning and growing, which results in their advancement.
f)   Filling vacancies from within the company is a cost-effective and time-saving option. Advertising, testing, or interviews aren't necessary because the qualifications of potential candidates are already well-established.

Demerits of Internal recruitment:
These difficulties are inherent in internal recruiting.

It's possible that current employees aren't adequately prepared for the new position. It's possible that the current personnel does not have the necessary skills.

b) There is no way to replace all of the openings internally. For entry-level positions, the company has to rely on outside sources.

As a result, internal applicants may lack originality and a new perspective on their work. Internal recruiting, therefore, is a breeding ground for new ideas.

d) This strategy reduces the number of options available and eliminates the chance for outsiders to show their worth.

External recruitment:

It is necessary to seek for external sources of recruiting. External sources are outside the scope of a particular issue. But it takes a lot of time and money to do so. External recruitment methods include: advertisements, employment exchanges, employment agencies etc.

1. **Advertising**: It is the most common method of attracting new employees from the outside. It is a simple and cost-effective solution for a wide range of workers. Adverts can provide candidates with all of the information they need to make an informed decision about whether or not they are a good fit. By providing a postbox number, the company can keep its true identity hidden if necessary.

2. **Educational Institutions:** The most common method of recruiting from the outside is through newspaper and journal advertisements. In terms of convenience and cost, this is an excellent option for a wide range of employees. The advertisement can provide a lot of information so that prospects can do their own self-screening. A post box number can be used to keep the company's identity a secret if necessary.

3. **Personnel Consultants:** A consulting firm is a company that specializes in helping clients find new employees. An middleman between the company and job searchers is provided by this service. It promotes the position and accepts applicants in response to a requirement from a client company. It can either forward the applications to the client firm, or it can perform tests

and interviews and charge the client company a fee. For the most part, this source is used to hire executives.

5. **Employment Exchanges** There is a lot of value in using public employment marketplaces to find new employees. These exchanges allow job searchers to register their names. Candidates who meet the requirements of a job posting are referred to employers by these exchanges.

7. **Unsolicited Applicants:** As a result of India's high unemployment rate, businesses receive a great number of unsolicited applicants at the front gate or via mail. In the event that an employer has a vacancy, these individuals may be put on a "waiting list" for future consideration.

Merit of External recruitment: a) If the company has a large number of applicants, it can choose the best among them.

b)   A fresh perspective: Candidates recruited from outside the organisation bring a distinct perspective. They don't have any built-in biases or prejudices.

c)   A wide range of knowledge: The company can secure candidates with a wide range of knowledge.

Demerits of External recruitment:

It's possible that some people who are brought in from outside will be unable to cope with the new environment. It's possible they're agitated, argumentative, or suspicious. In some cases, they may need to be finished and replaced.

Excluding the cost of advertising, testing, and interviewing applicants from outside the company, additional resources are required to hire and train new employees.

Employees who are hired from the outside are more likely to feel a sense of insecurity. Employees may not be willing to work with the company to the fullest extent.

SELECTION

"Selection is the process by which candidates are divided into two classes-those who will be offered employment and those who will not?"

"Selection is the process of choosing from among the candidates, from within the organization or from the outside, the most suitable person for the current position or for the future position."

The selection procedure splits the candidates into two groups: those who will be hired and those who will not be hired.." Due to the number of candidates being rejected, this process could be dubbed "rejection." Unsuitable candidates are culled from the pool. Selective hiring is frequently viewed as an undesirable practise, in contrast to the more positive aspect of hiring new employees.

SELECTION PROCESS

There is no one-size-fits-all method for determining which staff are most suited for a company's needs. Job to job, and company to company, the selecting process varies greatly. Selecting might be a straightforward one-step process in some circumstances. However, in many circumstances, it is extremely time-consuming and difficult to implement. These are the primary steps in the selection process:

Preliminary Interview: Candidates that are completely unsuited for the position are weeded out during the preliminary interview process. As a general rule, it's just a few minutes long and takes place in the company's employment office. As part of the application process, candidates are required to submit a brief profile that includes information about their age, education, experience, and interests. There is no need to spend money and time on those who aren't qualified, and the candidate doesn't have to deal with the lengthy application process. Preliminary interviews give an overview of a candidate's background. The candidate's application and curriculum vitae are important, but they aren't particularly effective in making final selection judgments.

Application Blank: Successful candidates will be asked to fill out a blank application form that will collect all the essential information. A number of application forms are used by various organisations and job opportunities. There should be as few steps as possible in the application. Data collection should only focus on what is needed for the task at hand. Information on a potential employee's personal history, educational background, work history, and references may all be included in a typical job application. This includes things like the applicant's full name, birth date, gender, marital status, and country of nationality. On the application blank, applicants can permanently record their schooling, work history, and interests in their own handwriting. It's a good approach to gain a sense of the candidate's suitability for the position. Thinking about interview questions, this is an excellent starting point. Shows the employer's interest in test candidates as well with the application blank, you may get all the information you need to know about a candidate's past.

Selection Tests: The use of tests in the hiring process has grown in importance in recent years. These are used to ensure that the job is done quickly and effectively. In practice, a variety of tests are utilized to measure the skills and abilities that are necessary for screening candidates. It is possible for written tests to be both descriptive and objective. Due to their difficulty in legal defense, personality tests are not widely used in job selection. However, they are regaining prominence, and chances are that employees will have to take personality tests at some time in their careers.

Employment Interview: The most common way for hiring new personnel is to have a face-to-face interview. During the interview, the employer and the candidate meet face to face. Compared to the initial interview, this one is more in-depth and comprehensive. During an interview for a job, the major goals are to verify the information gathered in previous steps, to learn more about the applicant, to assess their qualifications, and to provide background information on the position and the firm. When it comes to assessing a candidate's personality, interviewing is the best way to do it. However, the employment interview has a number of flaws. In the first place, an interview is a time-consuming and pricey tool. Secondly, an interview can only tell you about a person's personality, not about his or her ability to perform the job at hand.

Thirdly, the interview procedure relies too heavily on the personal opinion of the interviewers. Judgment errors and biases can lead to inaccurate outcomes. They may not be able to extract the information they need from the candidate. As a final point, interviews are often viewed as having more significance and validity than they actually do. The real man' may not be revealed by the answers to queries. Appearances can be deceiving. A competent interviewer may turn out to be a poor performer on the job.

Checking References: As a standard part of the application process, job candidates are asked for a list of referees who can speak to things like their educational background, work experience, skills and moral character. If the referee is knowledgeable and truthful, he might be a valuable source of information. He may be the candidate's former boss or a former professor. In order to gather more information about a candidate's abilities and integrity before making a final decision, the company may call the candidate's referees. The candidate may be asked for a letter of recommendation as well. Checking the references can reveal differences in a candidate's prior work, wage history, and reasons for leaving a position. Reference checks, on the other hand, are not very reliable in practise **Group Discussion:** To choose executives and civil workers, this strategy is becoming increasingly popular. Candidates are gathered together and given a topic to discuss using this approach. The interviewers keep a close eye on how each candidate contributes to the discussion from the rear of the room. Personality traits, communication skills, the ability to get along with people and accept the views of others, etc. can be discovered using this method. It's impossible for the candidate to pretend to be someone he's not. In the midst of a debate, his personality comes to the fore and reveals itself in his attitude and behaviour. Group discussions are evaluated to determine a person's direction and their ability to sell. Interaction analysis is the term for this type of investigation.

Physical Examination: To ensure that the candidate is physically fit for the position, a medical or physical examination is conducted. Checks on physical appearance and well-being might range from a simple assessment to a more extensive examination. Depending on the company, a candidate's medical certificate from a competent physician may be accepted. A fitness test conducted by an expert hired by the business is required of the candidate. Employees who undergo a thorough medical check can rest certain that they are in good health and have enough physical fitness. It will cut down on absenteeism, accidents, and turnover in the workplace. A complete medical checkup candidate has three purposes: first, it helps to determine the applicant's physical ability to satisfy the work requirement; second, it serves as a screening tool to ensure that the candidate is fit for the job. Because it prevents the spread of contagious illnesses, it is also beneficial for business. Third, it safeguards the company from bogus claims under the Worker's Compensation Act.

Final Approval: It is then possible to narrow the field down to a group of qualified applicants following the screening process. An email with the list is delivered to the manager who ordered the staff. The final decision rests with him. Appointment letters and service agreements are issued to the candidates who have been formally authorised by the manager in charge. Candidate probation periods range from one to two years. This is due to the fact that no method of selection is flawless. If an employee is judged unsuited during the probationary period, he or she may be transferred to a different position. As an alternative, he may be given time and training to improve his abilities. It's possible that he'll be fired if the company doesn't have a suitable position for him.

SELECTION TEST

A selection test is a method for systematic sampling of human behaviour. In other words, a selection test is a tool that enables and distinguishes an individual's expected and unexpected behaviour.

A test is a series of questions, exercises, or practical activities designed to assess an individual's aptitude, skill, or knowledge.

A selection test is a method that enables the identification of an individual's acquired human behaviour. The purpose of the selection exam must be as follows:

i.   It should forecast an individual's future performance.

ii.   It should be capable of diagnosing the underlying cause of specific behaviour.

iii.   It should be situational in nature..

SELECTION TESTS – VALIDATION

validity in a test assures equality, which means that all applicants are judged fairly; no candidate or group of candidates is subjected to unjustified prejudice.

1. Content Validity:

Such a test can be used to simulate the work that will be performed on the job; applicants can be given a representative sample of typing and their performance evaluated against that sample. Assuming that the work on the test is representative of actual job work, the test is content valid.

2. Construct Validity:

Construct validity refers to the degree to which a test assesses a specific trait associated with successful job performance.

3. Criterion-Related Validity:

The link between predictor and criterion is expressed as a validity coefficient, which theoretically ranges from +1.0 to -1.0, with the former exhibiting the highest positive coefficient and the latter exhibiting the largest negative coefficient. The greater the strength of the positive link, the more reliable the test.

4. Predictive Validity:

Predictive validity refers to the degree to which a test score correlates with a future desirable behaviour on the job. Predictive validity establishes the validity of a test through the use of potential applicants as a study group. The test is administered to all potential candidates despite its questionable validity.

At this level, candidates are hired based on a variety of previously used selection criteria. Their test scores, on the other hand, are retained as a safeguard. These personnel are evaluated on the basis of their actual job performance after a period of time, typically a year or more.

The assessment scores of each employee are compared to their test scores to determine the relationship between the test as a prediction and their actual job performance as a criteria. A high coefficient indicates that the test is valid. If the coefficient is small, the test is repeated. While this method is more expensive and time consuming, it is better since it establishes a relationship between the predictor and criterion on an empirical basis.

5. Concurrent Validity:

Concurrent validity is an alternative to predictive validity. It refers to the degree to which a test score is related to another measure of job behaviour that is accessible concurrently. Concurrent validation verifies a test by utilising current employees as subjects. To ascertain the relationship between the predictor and criterion, test scores are immediately matched to employees' actual performance data.

When the connection coefficient is large, the test is valid. However, concurrent validity raises numerous questions. It has been contested on the grounds that current employees are already familiar with the job and that learning takes time. When time and resources are not a consideration, a well-conducted concurrent validity study may be preferable to predictive validity.

The two validation approaches described above enable the collection of validation data from small samples of applicants or current employees in a particular position. As a result, they may not accurately reflect the diversity of potential personnel. To a certain extent, synthetic validity is the better option.

6. Synthetic Validity:

Synthetic validity refers to the process of validating a test by using components of numerous similar tasks rather than just one. Thus, validity is established by correlating predictor scores to the same job characteristic across multiple employers and aggregating the employees. For instance, a typing ability test might be evaluated against typing performance for not only typing clerks, but also for other workers that conduct typing labour in a company.

SELECTION TESTS – RELIABILITY

Personality traits that don't change over time can have an impact on the validity of a test, as opposed to knowledge and abilities that do. Test-retest, alternate form, and split halves approaches can be used to measure the dependability of a test.

ORIENTATION
CONCEPT

Orientation is the process of familiarising employees with the organization's regulations, job tasks and responsibilities, and other organisational characteristics and concepts that will aid them in settling into their new position efficiently. In larger organisations and for roles with increased responsibilities, orientation may include time spent in many departments as well as participation in specialised learning programmes.

The term orientation is synonymous with the term onboarding. While the phrases are technically similar, onboarding may imply a more robust experience that involves additional resources from the company and lays a higher emphasis on both intangible organisational culture and traditional norms and behaviours. The process may begin sooner (even before the new employee begins), conclude later, and use novel learning methods such as eLearning tools.

Orientation is a process by which employees are introduced to the organization's ideology, values, statistics, and information in order to help them acclimate to their new environment. It may refer to marketing or production orientation, employee or consumer orientation.

Orientation is frequently used to refer to the process of inducting new employees or acclimating existing employees to new technology, procedures, and rules in the workplace.

The selecting process's objective is orientation. Orientation is a process by which employees are introduced to the organization's ideology, values, statistics, and information in order to help them acclimate to their new environment. It may refer to marketing or production orientation, employee or consumer orientation.

PROCESS OF ORIENTATION

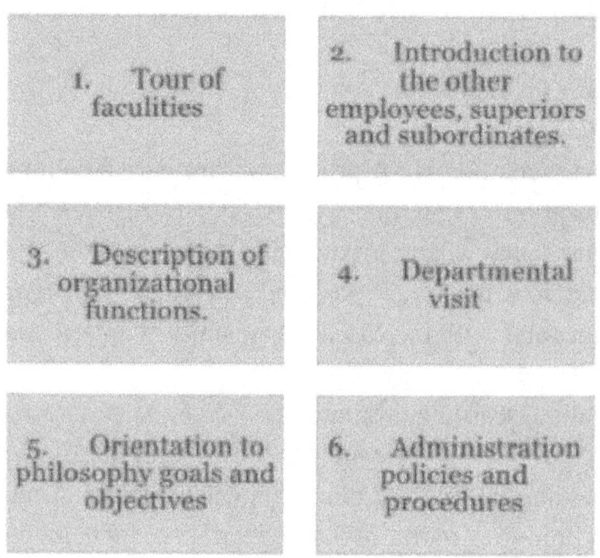

Reception:

Initially, the organisation extends a warm welcome to new employees. As new employees believe they have come here to accomplish a specific task, the business treats them with proper respect. This way, the organisation motivated new employees to perform better.

Acceptance stage:

The second stage of orientation is acceptance. At this level, employees have a favourable view toward their coworkers. A critical function is for colleagues to ensure that the work environment is adequate for proper performance.

Executive's personal interest:

Personal involvement on the part of executives indicates that they are personally interested in learning about the new personnel. So that new employees feel valued members of the organisation.

Introducing with colleagues:

The organisation acquaints new employees with their coworkers. By doing so, an organisation successfully establishes amicable and cordial relationships between new and existing personnel.

Introducing with supervisors:

This is a critical phase of orientation. This stage provides new employees with the opportunity to meet with senior management.

Introduce with service and regulation

Employees are introduced to the service's rules and regulations during this stage. If they have clear rules and regulations in place, they will all conduct their operations with caution.

Understanding the facilities

The organisation gives information to new employees on the advantages and facilities available to them during this stage of employment. By ensuring that these facilities' personnel have access to a quality of life. As a result, they attempt to impart their influence in order to ensure the work's success.

Follow-up

If any errors are discovered during the step analysis, those steps must be fixed. This is referred to as follow-up.

•

UNIT-4
CONCEPT OF TRAINING

Training is a planned activity aimed at enhancing performance on an individual, group, and/or organisational level. Improved performance, on the other hand, means that demonstrable changes in knowledge.

Training is about fostering an individual's development and assisting them in being more confident and competent in their lives and employment. The learning process is at the heart of training, and there are various and different methods and chances for learning.

TRAINING PROCESS

The Training Process is comprised of a set of procedures that must be followed in order to ensure the efficiency of the training programme. Training is a systematic activity that is used to modify an employee's abilities, attitudes, and behaviour in order to prepare them to do a certain job.

Identifying Training Needs:

The need of training is analyzed according to the requirement of the employees.

Establish Specific Objectives:

Define the training objectives. Primary goal of training is to ensure that man and work is a good match.

Select Appropriate Methods:

Techniques of instruction are desired methods of achieving training objectives.

Implement Programs:

The actual functioning begins with the selection of a suitable strategy.

Evaluate Program:

It entails an examination of numerous components of training in order to determine the effectiveness of the programme.

Feedback:

The collected data is then assessed and analysed in order to identify weak points in training programmes and make recommendations for future improvements.

TRAINING METHODS

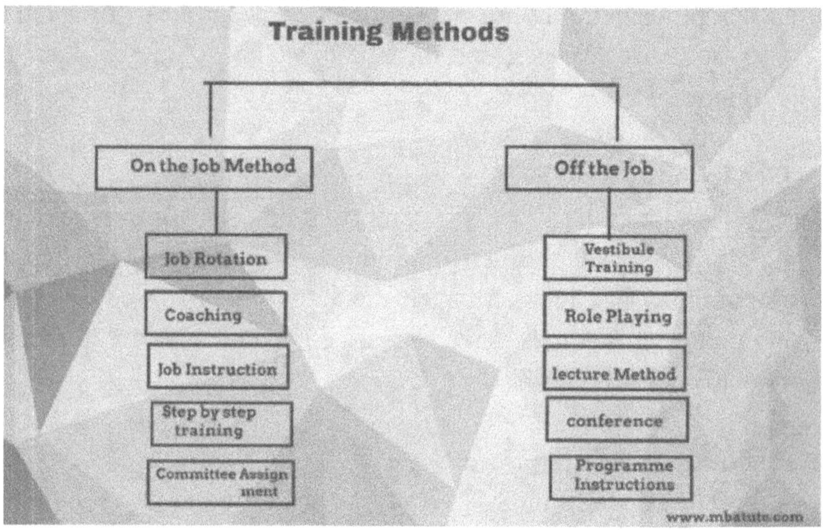

On the job training methods
1. Job Rotation

It entails the trainee's migration from one employment to another. From his supervisor or trainer, the trainee obtains job knowledge and experience.

2. Coaching

The supervisor evaluates the trainee's performance and makes suggestions for improvement.

3. Job Instruction

The trainer evaluates the trainees' performance, provides information, and corrects them.

4. Committee Assignment

This strategy assigns and challenges a group of trainees to solve a real-world organisational problem. The learners collaborate to tackle the problem and build collaboration skills.

Off the Job Methods
1. Vestibule training

This is the type of training that is used to prepare employees for clerical and semi-skilled occupations.

2 Role-Playing

It is defined as a technique for human connection that entails realistic behaviour in a fictitious environment.

3. Lecture Method

The lecture is a time-honored and straightforward technique of instruction. The instructor organises the content and delivers it in the form of a talk to a group of trainees. This is advantageous for instructing a large group of trainees.

4. Conference

It is a procedure for administrative, professional, and supervisory staff. This entails a group of people who present ideas, study and discuss data, hypotheses, and conclusions.

MANAGEMENT DEVELOPMENT
CONCEPT

Managers develop not only through official courses of instruction designed by the business, but also through on-the-job training. It should be understood that the organisation is responsible for developing its managers and potential managers.

The following are the essential assumptions and issues that underpin management development:

1. An executive must continue to grow throughout his or her work life and professional career. Thus, management development is a continuous process.
2. There is always a discrepancy between the'required performance level' and an individual's 'capacity.' Management must close the gap in order to provide a window of opportunity for progress.
3. Certain personal variables (such as age, habits, level of motivation, and state of mind, among others) hinder an individual's progress.
4. In the workplace, growth entails stresses and strains. Rarely can development occur in an entirely tranquil environment.
5. Engagement and participation are necessary components of growth.
6. In addition to the approach, there must be clearly defined objectives and goals to be accomplished.
7. Weaknesses must be identified. Feedback and counselling to junior colleagues, highlighting flaws and recommending appropriate human resource development tools to address them, are generally required.

However, an equal, if not more significant, counterpart to the organization's efforts are those of the individuals. Self-growth is a critical idea throughout the management development programme.

DEFINITIONS OF MANAGEMENT DEVELOPMENT

"Management development encompasses the process through which managers and executives gain not just the skills and competencies necessary to perform their current positions but also the capacities necessary to perform increasingly challenging and complex managerial duties in the future."

"Management development focuses on systematic growth of the managerial cadre's knowledge base, attitudes, fundamental skills, interpersonal skills, and technical abilities."

It assists managers in arming themselves with cutting-edge technology, tools, and procedures that result in increased quality and performance.

METHODS OF MANAGEMENT DEVELOPMENT
In Basket:

This method's coverage area is limited to the manager's incoming mail. The trainee is provided with a variety of business documents, including reports, notes, and telephone messages that would normally pass a manager's desk. The paper is given in an ad hoc manner. The learner is expected to take action in response to the information included in these documents. The first step in this strategy is to establish the importance of issues and then take appropriate action.

This procedure is straightforward, simple, and inexpensive. Although the selections are made quickly, the primary value is determined by the amount of feedback and reinforcement offered. The manager is forced to examine not only his administrative activities, but also his behavioural style, as a result of the feedback on his decisions.

Business Games:

Business games are classroom simulations in which teams of individuals compete against one another to accomplish a certain goal. These simulations try to replicate specific aspects of a situation, which participants then control. Participants are allocated roles like as president, controller, marketer, and manager, among others. They make judgments that affect the pricing level, the amount of manufacturing, and the inventory level.

Computer software manipulates the outcomes of their actions, simulating those of a real-world business setting. Participants get an understanding of how their actions affect other groups and vice versa. These simulations are designed to teach trainees how to make integrated management decisions. They provide to a better understanding of the intricate relationships that exist between organisational units.

Though developing business games is a relatively challenging and expensive task. Taylor and Lippit (1975) stated that "trainees nearly always respond positively to a well-run game, and it is an effective strategy for improving problem-solving and leadership skills."

Sensitivity Training:

This method was invented by Kurt Lenin and popularised by the National Training Laboratories in the United States of America under the leadership of Leland Broadford. This technique is based on the premise that change in behaviour cannot occur solely via information. Practice in human relations provides an environment conducive to changing attitudes and approaches.

"Sensitivity Training is a group experience aimed to expose people' behaviour, provide and receive feedback, experiment with new behaviours, and build awareness of self and others."

The purpose of this training is to develop an awareness of oneself and sensitivity to others; the ability to listen to others and communicate a diagnostic understanding of group problems; the ability to contribute effectively and appropriately to group work; and an appreciation for the complexities of intergroup and intra-organizational problems. The most frequently used methodology is for small groups of eight to twelve people to gather in an unstructured learning scenario away from the workplace.

The trainer's role is to function as a catalyst. He provides group members to openly express their thoughts and feelings using the group's own procedures. Individuals are free to concentrate on their behaviour rather than their responsibilities. Each group member is encouraged to express his or her thoughts and perceptions about others in the group. The emphasis is on direct confrontation and interaction.

"Because of its nature," Mathis (1990) comments, "the sensitivity training group is a contentious approach." According to others, this is unethical, unworkable, and harmful." Simultaneously, this training increases empathy for others' concerns and interpersonal competency in dealing with relationships and problem solving. It's an excellent team-building activity. As a result, the organization's performance and profitability improve.

Understudy:

The chief of a given department may select an understudy. It enables the superior to alleviate some of his workload by delegating some of his duties to a designated individual. This activity will be effective only if trainees are given genuine opportunities to work on difficult or fascinating assignments rather than executing paper shuffling chores. The understudy approach also eliminates the possibility of making an expensive error; nonetheless, this method does suffer from some favoritism on the part of superiors throughout the selection process.

Multiple Management:

Additionally, it is referred to as a Junior Board of Executives. In this strategy, the Chief Executive of the organisation forms advisory committees of junior level executives to investigate the organization's challenges and give recommendations to upper management. This provides juniors with an opportunity to participate in managerial decision-making and to learn through observation.

PERFORMANCE MANAGEMENT CONCEPT

Performance management is a comprehensive, highly interactive, and goal-oriented technique for managing and overseeing managers in the workplace. It is defined as a thorough, planned technique to controlling and rewarding performance through the building and maintenance of positive manager (employee) motivation. Its key dimensions are performance standards - which outline the organization's aims and objectives - as well as management recognition and reward.

PERFORMANCE MANAGEMENT METHODS
Graphic Rating Scale Method

Supervisors utilize this strategy to assess employee performance the most frequently. This graphical scale can be used to evaluate numerous team members at the same time, utilizing numerical or text values ranging from terrible to excellent. In the context of a team, an employee's abilities, competence, behaviour, and other traits might be assessed. Making each employee aware of the scale's worth in terms of success and failure is critical. It would be wonderful if this scale was the same for everyone.

An employee's specific attributes are rated using this method. A company's decision-making and emotional stability, for example, may be used to assess an employee's capacity to balance quality and quantity of labour.

Graphic scales are useful, cost-effective, and rapid to develop. They also aid in achieving a specific goal more successfully. As a result, an individual's assessment of a situation can vary greatly. Inconsistencies in evaluations could arise as a result of this. Personal bias can also come into play. Each character must be defined as clearly as possible.

2. Ranking Method

The name of this strategy explains exactly what it is. Human Resources assign a numerical value to each employee based on a set of criteria established by the department. Hence, the best performers are on the top, and the worst performers rank at the bottom.

There are numerous ways to customise this straightforward system for assigning staff rankings. Using a paired comparison ranking technique, employees are ranked against one another in pairs of two. We keep track of how many times one employee is given preference over another. The top employee is the one with the largest number of preferences.

3. Checklist Method

A checklist is used to evaluate employees in this manner. There are a number of elements that might be included in the checklist, depending on what the HR department considers important. Employees' performance is then rated depending on the selections made by employers in the checkboxes.

A numerical value is assigned to each item on the checklist based on its significance to job performance. When all of these elements are taken into account, the overall appraisal score is determined.

Behaviour-based evaluations, for example, are carried out using a checklist. Having predetermined personality and behavioural markers is the key to this. If an employee fits these criteria, they will be considered for an evaluation if they meet them.

The checklist technique makes it simple for managers to evaluate their staff because they only have to answer "yes" or "no." It also makes it easier for employees to get clear and immediate feedback. Even so, designing an effective checklist and assigning a weight to each factor may not be straightforward.

4. Management by Objectives Method (MBO)

The term "management by objectives" refers to a method of performance evaluation that is universally accepted and widely used (MBO). Using this strategy, you are evaluating your staff based on their performance. For more than just performance evaluation, MBO provides a framework for managing the entire company. Vision, values, strategies, goals and performance evaluation are all included in the breadth of the organization's vision.

At the top of a corporation, managers establish the organization's objectives. It's at this point that lower-level supervisors and staff set their own goals. Employees' objectives are aligned with those of their supervisors. These goals are pursued by the entire organization as a whole.

Newly motivated and focused employees return to work following a meeting with their bosses to set short- and long-term objectives. Their managers monitor their employees' performance, provide coaching and assistance, eliminate barriers or assist employees in overcoming them, and make modifications and course corrections as necessary. Every step of the way, the employees' performance and progress are documented, measured, and transparent.

As a result, managers and their staff are able to create stronger ties. There is a lot of face-to-face interaction between managers and employees in MBO, which encourages camaraderie and communication, as well as trust in the workplace. • It creates an atmosphere of trust and cooperation. MBO fosters a climate of mutual respect and trust both within and outside of a single department.

As a result of direct communication between management and employees, MBO increases the quality of decisions and problem solutions

5. 360-degree Feedback Appraisal

Employees are evaluated based on the progress they have achieved both within and outside of their own team in this performance evaluation approach. In addition to evaluations from direct supervisors and immediate peers, inputs from supervisors in other departments are taken into account. Each employee receives a rating based on their own performance as well as the performance of the team in which they are a member.

FACTORS THAT DISTORT PERFORMANCE APPRAISAL
1. Leniency error

Each evaluator has his own value system which works as a benchmark against which appraisals are performed. Some assessors place a high value on an individual's performance, while others place a low value on it.

2. Halo error

Halo error or halo effect is a tendency to grade high or low on all variables due to the impression of a high or poor rating on some specific element.

3. Low appraiser motivation

If the evaluator understands that a low rating could affect the employee's future, say, possibilities for advancement, the evaluator may be reluctant to deliver a genuine appraisal.

CAREER PLANNING

Career planning is a continuous process by which an individual defines his career goals and determines the means and techniques to achieve them. Career planning refers to the process of making long-term decisions about one's career. In order to achieve career fulfilment, it motivates and, in some cases, drives a person to investigate, select, and strive. Hence has significance in individual's existence.

CAREER STAGES

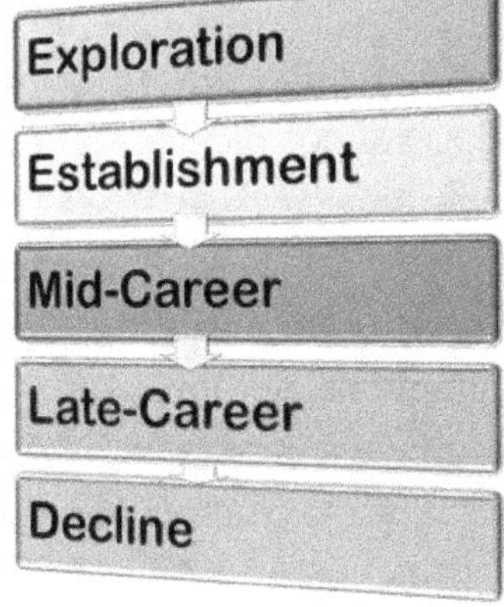

Exploration:

The exploration period is the pre-employment stage, whereby the individuals are in their mid-twenties and enter from their college life to the job world. The individuals narrow down their employment selections on the basis of the guidance offered by their parents, friends, family, teachers.

Establishment

This is the time when a person gets a firsthand look at what it's like to work at his or her first office. Here, all the expectations and fantasies come to an end, and one has to confront the reality of life. This period encompasses around 10 years from the 25 years of age.

Mid-Career:

Ages 35 to 45 years old are considered to be the prime of life in this stage. At this stage, the individual is no longer considered to be a fresher and his blunders are taken seriously by the senior management.

Late-Career

As a result of the growth or stagnation in their career graphs, an individual can attain a specific position in the organisational hierarchy during this stage.

If a person continues to develop professionally even after the mid-career stage (i.e. 20 years after the mid-forties), it is believed that he or she is having a positive work experience. In this situation, one person assumes the role of mentor and helps others learn from his or her own experiences.

Decline: This is the last stage of career development. At this stage, an individual has to step out of his work or get a retirement from his official commitments.

Thus, every individual passes through these five stages of career development as they move along their life cycle.

CAREER ANCHORS

Career Anchors are the aspects of a role, profession or career that individuals are pulled to. In most cases, they're in line with how an individual sees his or her abilities, motivations, and ideals. Finding one's career anchors might be made easier with a career anchors activity.

COMPENSATION
MEANING

The amount of money an employee is paid for the services they provide to the company is referred to as compensation.

Human resource management relies on compensation to keep employees engaged and productive, which in turn helps the business run more efficiently.

Compensation has a direct impact on a number of organisational outcomes, including employee well-being, employee attraction, employee retention, job performance, skill development, teamwork, and adaptability.

Payroll-related compensation includes reimbursement, incentive payments, and strategic decisions about how salaries and wages are administered. Salary, salaries, commissions, and bonuses are all examples of direct monetary compensation.

All the things that employee gets in return for his or her labour, including as wages, salaries, allowances, benefits, and services, are included in the broad phrase "compensation".

STEPS IN DETERMINING COMPENSATION
Determine Sales Force and Compensation Objectives:

The sales manager should establish the business objectives and also the objectives of the salespeople while developing a pay plan.

Determine Major Compensation Issues:

Wage levels, wage structures, salesperson salaries, and salary administration procedures all have a role in determining the most important aspects of a worker's compensation.

Salary is compared to the remuneration of the sales force of competitors when determining wage levels of compensation for that sales force. A company's salespeople will always prefer to work for a competitor that pays a higher compensation, and the competitor will do the same for them, potentially resulting in a loss of staff for the company. Salary levels in the business can be used to compare compensation for different types of salespeople.

A salesperson's unique wage is determined by a variety of factors, including his or her level of experience, the nature of the profession, and his or her personal history. His abilities connected to work descriptions are considered while deciding on the compensation structure.

It's important to have a system in place to evaluate and control the sales force, as well as a way to modify compensation and make pay adjustments and raises that will encourage salespeople to stick around. Considering the organization's ability and desire to compensate its employees through salary, commissions, benefits, bonuses, and other forms of compensation, the sales manager creates a budget for paying the sales team.

Implement Long-Term and Short-Term Compensation Plans:

The sales compensation plan should be viewed from the perspective of the sales manager both in the short and long term. While in the near term, it should handle the issues of proper compensation and low cost drive for the firm, in the long-term, it should lower the attrition rate and develop people to take up higher tasks including managerial duties.

The component of the salesperson's employment that aids the company in reaching its objectives should be included in the pay message. The sales supervisor should also advise them about the role of the salespeople in reaching the sales objectives.

Employees must be made aware by their supervisors that their pay is directly tied to their skill and willingness to work toward the company's goals. If the salespeople devote themselves to the organisation and their performance improves, so also will be the sales of the organisation and consequently the level of compensation for the salespeople.

Relate Rewards to Performance:

Rewards are always tied to sales achievement in a compensation plan and communication strategy that have been scientifically created. Each level of the performance and reward system should be related to the contribution made by an individual salesperson to the organisation at this point in the compensation process.

It also establishes a direct link between a salesperson's success and their compensation by utilising an objective and rational means of assessing their performance.

Measurement of Performance:

Evaluation procedures, like the compensation plan, should be unbiased and open to the public. Sales organisations need to measure the performance of the salespeople occasionally.

Appraise the Compensation Plan:

It is vital to look at the redundancy effect of the compensation scheme. This should be done on a frequent basis so that the sales manager may find out the relevance of the company's com-pensation plan in the light of competition and evolutions in the sales management function.

JOB EVALUATION
CONCEPT

Employer-employee relations can be maintained and improved by focusing on wages and salaries. In order for an organization to recruit and retain top personnel, it must have a well-structured compensation plan that also ensures a happy and productive workforce. It is one of the most challenging tasks of management to set monetary base compensation rates. It is equally vital for employees to select the optimum compensation because it influences their status in society in terms of their lifestyle and level of living. Rate and salary administration programmes are designed to ensure that each employee receives a fair wage for the work he or she performs for their employer. Accordingly, job evaluation is an effort to determine the work's relative value. A process that can be used even by a human resources manager to come up with compensation plans.

(a) The job description.

(b) The current value of the job in comparison to other jobs in the area.

(c) The individual's ability to do the job well.

The first two variables are strongly linked to the evaluation of the job and the third to the evaluation of performance. Most compensation decisions are based on the comparison of a job's pay to other employment in the same or a similar position in another company. To make this comparison, we use Job assessment. While assessing a work's value is vital, it is important to remember that the evaluation is focused on the job itself, not the person doing it. Job evaluation presumes that the worker is performing the job to its full potential. As a result, the process of evaluating a job fails to take into account the unique qualities of the employee. Establishing a good wage and salary structure is made possible by conducting a job appraisal. In the process of evaluating a worker's ability to perform a given job, an attempt is made to determine and compare the demands that a typical worker would make when doing so. Assigning points or using other systematic ways for fundamental work needs such as abilities, experience and responsibility can be used to achieve the evaluation Rather than determining a job's price, it sets its relative value. It's an attempt to assess the relative worth of each job in a factory and establish what a reasonable starting wage should be for that job. It's not a way to judge the quality of the task being performed by the person performing it. Only the job itself is rated, and not the particular worker's abilities.

DEFINITIONS OF JOB EVALUATION

"Job evaluation is an attempt to determine and compare demands which the typical performance of a certain job makes on normal workers without taking into account the individual performance of the workers concerned".

"Job Evaluation is the application of the Job Analysis technique to the qualitative measurement of relative job worth, for the purpose of creating consistent wage rate differentials by objective means. It measures the differences between jobs on the job criteria, and establishes the differential numerically (job rating), so that it may be translated to wage rate after the wage level is determined".

To estimate the reasonable basic wage for a job, "Position Evaluation represents an effort to determine the relative value of each job in a factory."

"Job Evaluation as a personal term has both a particular and genetic meaning specifically, it implies job rating or the grading of jobs in terms of duties, and generally it signifies the entire field of salaries and salary administration along current lines".

In order to assess a job's value in comparison to other jobs, "Job Evaluation" is a methodical and organised process.

"Job Evaluation is a technique of analysing the worth of a job in comparison with all other positions throughout an organisation".

SALARY PAY STRUCTIURE

1. Basic Salary

It is the taxable base income and often not more than 40 percent of CTC. Many times, the wage structure is built around the basic salary.

Components can be expressed as a percentage of an employee's base compensation in most cases.

2. House Rent Allowance

The HRA constitutes 40 to 50 percent of the basic salary.

3. Special Allowances

Makes up for the rest part of the salary, generally smaller than the basic income and entirely taxed.

4. Leave Travel Allowance

Also referred to as LTA. The non- taxable sum paid by the company to the employee for vacation/trips with family.

5. Gratuity

In essence, it is a one-time payment made by an employer to a departing employee upon their resignation or retirement from their position.

6. Provident Fund

Funds set aside in case of an emergency or for later use by the retiree. 12 percent of the base wage is automatically withdrawn and goes to the employee provident fund.

7. Medical Allowance

The employer pays the employee for the medical expenditures incurred. Up to Rs.15, 000 of your purchase is tax-free.

8. Bonus

This is a taxable portion of the CTC that the company awards to each employee at the end of each year based on his or her individual and the company's performance.

FACTORS INFLUENCING COMPENSATION LEVELS
1. Years of experience and education level

It should go without saying that the more education and experience a candidate has, the more money they may anticipate to make. You need to be ready and willing to compensate appropriately if you want to attract job candidates with advanced degrees or more than five years of experience.

2. Industry

Depending on the business, workers with comparable or even the same job title can expect to make significantly different amounts of money. This disparity may be due to a variety of factors, such as the importance of the job function to a particular industry or the fact that one industry is significantly larger than the others.

3. Location

Cost of living, a crucial issue to consider when determining remuneration, is mostly reliant on geography and, more specifically, the cost of housing. A major part of the pay gap between urban and rural areas can be explained by the greater cost of living. Because of the rise of remote work, several companies have begun paying employees based on performance rather than geography.

TRENDS IN COMPENSATION MANAGEMENT

New ways of compensating employees are appearing alongside the emergence of new businesses. The purpose of this study is to determine the latest trends in sales force compensation and the ramifications for today's sales leadership. Changing trends in compensation can be divided into four broad groups. The most significant development has been the shift toward a pay model centred on maximising customer happiness.

The technology improvements have transformed the horizon of customer handling by the salesmen. In the past, salesmen had to go door-to-door to meet with each customer to provide the information they requested. Today, email management systems, broadband technology, videoconferencing, and other Web-based technologies enable the salesperson to respond to the customer's rising and evolving information requirement easier and faster.

The consumers are also delighted with the non- personal method of connection with the salesmen as it leads to lower cost of service and minimal intrusion by the salesperson at the customer's location. Because of the e-commerce platform, the buyer-seller dialogue is now more interactive and less obstructive.

This has made the sales profession more target-oriented, as salespeople now can concentrate more on real sales activities than on feeding current clients with important market knowledge, and thus, it has led to a rise in their remuneration level due to higher sales realisation.

Additionally, finding sales representatives from diverse nations who can all work together in the same office is a difficult task. A salary paid to an Indian working in the United States at the Indian rate may not be adequate for a European executive in India. People working in various countries or economic zones must also have their pay scales equalised.

Compensation plans should be seen as equitable across the organisation. It is noted that the wage structure is low at the base level where the real sales happens and grows higher as one moves farther from the customers to the upper hierarchy levels of the firm. This is a developing tendency that could obstruct the expansion of numerous firms.

Equal pay for equal work at all levels of the sales organisation should be a goal. In many sales, organisations the usual Indian salary is not equitable from numerous points of view, including gender disparity.

Many companies pay male and female employees differently, despite the fact that they do equivalent tasks. For a compensation plan that is both successful and equitable, management should be on the lookout for these kinds of inequalities and work to eliminate them.

INCENTIVE – MEANING

An incentive gives increased money for those employees who perform well. Employee productivity is used as a metric to determine whether or not they should receive greater compensation.

Anything that can grab an employee's attention and urge them to work can be considered as incentive. Increasing an organization's overall performance is the goal of an incentive. Incentives can be categorised as direct and indirect remuneration. Individual plans, group plans, and organisational plans can all be created.

INCENTIVES – IMPORTANCE

1. Workers are motivated to work more efficiently and produce more if they are given incentives..
2. The dread of instability in the minds of employees is eliminated when they are paid a fixed salary (as incentive as a part of total remuneration)
3. As a result of the incentive, employee earnings would rise.
4. Incentives to reduce the overall and unit costs of production (because of higher productivity)
5. Additionally, it is expected that production capacity will be increased.
6. Increased employee productivity and reduced absenteeism can be achieved through the use of incentive payments.

TYPES OF INCENTIVES

Incentives for Employees:

The following are the different incentives for employees which the company can use:

a. Financial Incentives:

The various financial incentives are:

(i) Pay and allowances

(ii) Productivity linked wage incentive

(iii) Bonus

(iv) Co-partnership/stock option

(v) Retirement benefits

(vi) Perquisites

b. Non-Financial Incentives:

The various non-financial incentives are:

(i) Employee recognition programmes

(ii) Employee empowerment

(iii) Job security

(iv) Status

(v) Employee participation

(vi) Organizational climate

BENEFITS

Benefits are an important element of a worker's compensation, and they can be extremely valuable to them.

Healthcare: health insurance is the most common form of perk, many employers also provide employees with access to onsite fitness facilities and stress-relieving programmes.

Retirement: Retirement schemes give employees monthly income when they leave the company. Even if a job isn't all that exciting, having a secure retirement is enough of an incentive for many people to continue with it.

Social security- Social insurance is a system in which employees and employers pay into a pool on a regular basis, either with or without government assistance. Benefits are provided to the contributors from these donations so that they can meet their basic needs in old age, sickness, unemployment, and other life calamities.

•

UNIT-5
PERFORMANCE EVALUATION AND CONTROL PROCESS

In order to monitor and evaluate employee performance on a regular basis, all firms that have mastered the art of "winning from within" rely on a systematized process of performance review. As a best practice, employees should be rated annually on their work anniversary based on which they are either promoted or given the appropriate amount of compensation raises. Employees benefit from regular feedback on their performance indicators when it is part of the performance review process.

The importance of conducting performance reviews cannot be overstated, despite the fact that they might be challenging. Organizations can use this information to see if their ways of selecting new employees are effective.

Training, development, and motivational programmes show where they're needed, and these programmes can then be used to evaluate whether they've been successful.

Performance evaluations are used by managers to determine pay, promotion, and dismissal for employees.

DEFINITION OF PERFORMANCE EVALUATION

According to a wide range of people, performance evaluation can signify many different things. Observation, judgment, and feedback are all part of the process of measuring.

It is a tool that the organization uses to achieve its set objectives.

Performance is defined as an employee's ability to complete given duties. It's all about getting the work done well the first time.

For managers, performance evaluation involves comparing the conduct of employees to established criteria, documenting the results, and providing feedback to employees about where and why they need to improve their performance.

It is an all-encompassing development tool for both the person and the company. There are many aspects to consider, including job expertise and output quality as well as leadership and supervisory skills as well as dependability, co-workers' cooperation and judgement as well as their versatility and health. Additionally, evaluation should be based on both the past and the future.

It is a system for assessing and evaluating the performance of an individual or a team in the workplace. A successful system evaluates achievements and develops strategies for future growth.

"Performance evaluation is the systemic evaluation of the individual respect for this performance on the job and his potential for development."

"Performance evaluation means evaluating an employee's current and/or past performance relative to his performance standards."

"Performance evaluation is the process by which organizations evaluate individual job performance."

PERFORMANCE EVALUATION METHODS

There are a number of key approaches for evaluating performance. While relying just on one of these performance evaluation methods can provide an organization with only one-sided information, a multi-method approach can provide a more complete picture, allowing for an unbiased and performance-centric conclusion.

SELF-EVALUATION

You can begin employee reviews with this strategy. Using multiple-choice or open-ended questions, an employee is asked to rate themselves based on a set of evaluation criteria. Management can fairly evaluate an employee's performance by taking into account the employee's perceptions of their own performance after they have completed a self-evaluation.

360-DEGREE EMPLOYEE EVALUATION

Employees are evaluated based on the progress they have achieved both within and outside of their own team in this performance evaluation approach. In addition to evaluations from direct supervisors and immediate peers, inputs from supervisors in other departments are taken into account. Each employee receives a rating based on their own performance as well as the performance of the team in which they are a member.

GRAPHICS RATING SCALE

Supervisors utilize this strategy to assess employee performance the most frequently. This graphical scale can be used to evaluate numerous team members at the same time, utilizing numerical or text values ranging from terrible to excellent. In the context of a team, an employee's abilities, competence, behaviour, and other traits might be assessed. Making each employee aware of the scale's worth in terms of success and failure is critical. It would be wonderful if this scale was the same for everyone.

An employee's specific attributes are rated using this method. A company's decision-making and emotional stability, for example, may be used to assess an employee's capacity to balance quality and quantity of labour.

Graphic scales are useful, cost-effective, and rapid to develop. They also aid in achieving a specific goal more successfully. As a result, an individual's assessment of a situation can vary greatly. Inconsistencies in evaluations could arise as a result of this. Personal bias can also come into play. Each character must be defined as clearly as possible.

CHECKLIST METHOD

A checklist is used to evaluate employees in this manner. There are a number of elements that might be included in the checklist, depending on what the HR department considers important. Employees' performance is then rated depending on the selections made by employers in the checkboxes.

A numerical value is assigned to each item on the checklist based on its significance to job performance. When all of these elements are taken into account, the overall appraisal score is determined.

Behaviour-based evaluations, for example, are carried out using a checklist. Having predetermined personality and behavioural markers is the key to this. If an employee fits these criteria, they will be considered for an evaluation if they meet them.

The checklist technique makes it simple for managers to evaluate their staff because they only have to answer "yes" or "no." It also makes it easier for employees to get clear and immediate feedback. Even so, designing an effective checklist and assigning a weight to each factor may not be straightforward.

RANKING METHOD

Employees can be ranked in many different ways using this easy system. Employees are ranked in pairs against each other using the paired comparison ranking methodology. All the times one employee has been chosen as the preferred choice over another is kept in the system. The employee with the most preferences is the best one.

Ratings and grades can be used together. On a scale of one to ten, the employees with the highest total grade rank first. Due to its simplicity and efficiency, the ranking technique has been deemed the most effective. Objective appraisal can be disrupted by bias and favouritism, however.

CRITICAL INCIDENT METHOD

Criticized occurrences were used to evaluate an employee's performance by pinpointing and detailing particular instances in which the individual performed well or needed improvement. Although it is sometimes used in conjunction with a grading system, it is an approach that relies solely on the description of the event.

Recording significant incidents may be encouraged by some bosses (where the employee excelled, situations that did not go well). In this case, the employee is more responsible and the management is not need to have been there when the incident happened.

Generally speaking, occurrences should be documented as soon as possible, rather than waiting until the end of the year for a performance assessment. When crucial event reports (good or bad) are not recorded in a timely manner, they suffer from a lack of detail and accuracy.

MBO

The term "management by objectives" refers to a method of performance evaluation that is universally accepted and widely used (MBO). Using this strategy, you are evaluating your staff based on their performance. For more than just performance evaluation, MBO provides a framework for managing the entire company. Vision, values, strategies, goals and performance evaluation are all included in the breadth of the organization's vision.

At the top of a corporation, managers establish the organization's objectives. It's at this point that lower-level supervisors and staff set their own goals. Employees' objectives are aligned with those of their supervisors. These goals are pursued by the entire organization as a whole.

Newly motivated and focused employees return to work following a meeting with their bosses to set short- and long-term objectives. Their managers monitor their employees' performance, provide coaching and assistance, eliminate barriers or assist employees in overcoming them, and make modifications and course corrections as necessary. Every step of the way, the employees' performance and progress are documented, measured, and transparent.

As a result, managers and their staff are able to create stronger ties. There is a lot of face-to-face interaction between managers and employees in MBO, which encourages camaraderie and communication, as well as trust in the workplace. • It creates an atmosphere of trust and cooperation. MBO fosters a climate of mutual respect and trust both within and outside of a single department.

As a result of direct communication between management and employees, MBO increases the quality of decisions and problem solutions.

PERFORMANCE FEEDBACK

Performance feedback is the continual process between employee and the manager when information is shared concerning the performance expected and the performance displayed.

INDUSTRY PRACTICES

Define and describe each role

Role of each employee working in an organization is clearly defined.

Pair goals with a performance plan

Develop a performance plan to go alongside with the goal.

Build a performance-aligned culture

Make sure your organisation has common values and cultural alignment. A sense of shared values, beliefs and expectations among employees produces a more harmonious and enjoyable workplace

PROMOTION

Promoting someone to a higher position entails increasing their workload, increasing their responsibilities and elevating their prestige. If it's related to the pay raise, it might or might not be.

One of the best ways to motivate employees is to give them more responsibility, a raise in pay, and a boost in morale and job satisfaction. Almost all employees want to grow in their careers, and promotion is a step up in the organization's hierarchy.

"A promotion involves a change from one job to another that is better in terms of status and responsibilities."

"A promotion is the transfer of an employee to a job that pays more money or that enjoys some better status."

"Promotion is an advancement of an employee to a better job, better in terms of greater responsibilities, more prestige or status, greater skill and specially increased rate of pay or salary".

"A promotion includes a transition from one position to another that is better in terms of status and responsibilities."

TYPES OF PROMOTIO

Horizontal Promotion:

Horizontal promotion occurs when an employee gets promoted to a new position in the same department, but with a higher salary, more duties, and a new title. For example, a First Division Assistant is promoted from a Second Division Assistant position. Within the same department, or between departments, or even between plants, this form of promotion is commonplace.

Vertical Promotion:

The term "vertical promotion" refers to the process through which a person moves up in rank and responsibilities while also receiving a raise in salary and other benefits. A sales manager, for example, may be promoted to the position of general manager in his or her organization.

Dry Promotion:

"Dry promotion" refers to a promotion without an increase in income or remuneration. Taking the example of a university professor who was elevated to the position of department head but received no pay raise. There will be a change in title and responsibilities, but no change in compensation, in a dry promotion.

PURPOSE OF PROMOTION

1. The act of recognising and rewarding an individual's efforts.
2. To retain and reward an employee for his unbroken continuous service to the organisation.

3. To improve a worker's contribution to the company's success.
4. To promote loyalty morale, and belongingness on the part of the employee.
5. In order to improve morale and productivity among the workforce.
6. To find and hire employees that is both qualified and interested in working for the company.
7. It forms critical to have a promotion system in place because it rewards initiative, enterprise, and ambition while also reducing employee dissatisfaction and unrest. It also serves to attract and retain highly qualified employees while also requiring a system of logical training for advancement.

DEMOTION

When an employee is demoted, he or she is transferred to a position with a lesser level of salary, responsibilities, or prestige. Demotion seldom holds favourable effects for the individual.

When a person is demoted, it's usually because of poor work performance or inappropriate behaviour, including being absent too much or being inept.

When a pay cut doesn't work, the employees are demoted. In a demotion, an employee's existing position is reduced by one level. It's a given that the employee will have a bad view of the company because it's a long-term situation. Because of this, demotions should only be attempted after careful consideration. Consider taking action if the organization is confident that the employee will not resign or reduce work performance, and if the action will not have a harmful long-term effect. If you've been demoted, you'll lose both your position and your income and benefit package. Because of this, there is a great chance that employees will never be happy with the company again.

TRANSFER

People or money can be transferred from one location to another using the verb "transfer." It is a frequent word used in the field of human resource which implies the migration of personnel from one position to another. Employees of the same grade were frequently transferred at a later date.

Employment transfer is the shift of job for employees; the change might be in terms of site of job, department of job or shift of job. The personnel are replaced or relocated lateral to serve the best for the organisation.

TYPE OF TRANSFER

Production Transfers:

These are transfers done from one department or plant to the other department or plant where there are labour surpluses or shortage. Not having enough workers in one part of the company while having a need for workers in another part of the company is a bad thing. So, production transfer helps to stabilise the employment in the company.

Replacement Transfers:

These are comparable to production transfers as these are also meant to avoid lay-offs, especially of senior staff. A senior employee can take the place of a new hire in order to prevent the older employee from being laid off.

Remedial Transfers:

These are comparable to production transfers as these are also meant to avoid lay-offs, especially of senior staff. To keep the senior employee from being laid off, a new employee may be replaced by another senior employee.

Versatility Transfers:

These are meant to make an individual more competent and adaptable by transferring him from one job to another. In this method, a person learns new abilities and receives more and broader job experience. Additionally, they aid in the employee's potential for promotion in the company.

Shift Transfers:

When the industrial establishments are functioning in more than one shift then shift transfers are conducted. An employee is switched from one shift to another on the same work. These transfers are performed on rotation basis.

SEPARATION

Employment separation refers to the conclusion of an employee's employment connection with a corporation. This might happen when an employment contract or an at-will arrangement between an employer and an employee ends. While occasionally the employer makes the decision to end employment, an employee may also begin a voluntary employment separation if they choose to retire or resign.

Separation indicates end of service of agreement with the organisation.

RESIGNATION

A resignation refers to the termination of employment at the instance of the employee in that case it is voluntary but if forced by the employer for not putting his duty well ,or for some serious charge against him than it becomes involuntary. An employee may resign when he or she gets a good job elsewhere, or due to ill health, or may resign due to some personal problems.

VOLUNTARY RETIREMENT SCHEME

Voluntary retirement scheme VRS sometimes referred to as the "golden hand shake plan" has been used by both public and private sector employers since the early 1980s to send home surplus workers for good reasons instead of retrenchment. The departing staff is given generous severance packages. To reduce the size of the workforce and get rid of employees who are no longer productive, VRS is recommended as a quick and easy solution. Many companies, such as Hindustan Lever, Siemens, and TISCO, have had considerable success with this programme.

RETRENCHMENT

It refers to the termination of an employee due to the employment of machines to substitute human labour or the closing of a department due to a lack of demand for the items created in that department. Management and personnel must leave the plant if it is shut down, and they must do so immediately. Section 25(f) of the Industrial Discrimination Act, 1947 states that employees who are laid off or terminated are entitled to compensation equal to 15 days' average wage for every year they have worked continuously. When an employee is laid off, they are still employed by the company and can be recalled at the end of their layoff time. However, when an employee is retreived, their employment is terminated instantly. Retaining employees is also different from sacking them. Due to an employee's own fault, he or she is fired, but retrenchment is a situation where both the company and the employee are compelled to terminate a large number of employees.

LAYOFF

A layoff is a temporary separation of an employee from their employer. Industrial Disputes Act, 1947 Section 2(kkk) defines layoff as "the failure, refusal or incapacity of an employer to employ a worker whose name is present on the rolls but whose position has not been retrenched." It is possible for an employee to be laid off for a predetermined amount of time, after which time they will be called back to work by their employer. Employees who have been let go by their employers are entitled to back pay for the time they were unemployed. According to Section 25 of the Industrial Disputes Act, 1947, employers must compensate employees for all days they were laid off. The compensation must be equal to half of the typical wages the employee would have earned if he or she had not been laid off. Layoffs can be caused by any of the following:

Coal, power, or raw material shortages.

A rise in inventory

Machinery malfunctions, for example.

DISMISSAL

When an employer determines that retaining a worker is no longer in the best interest of the company, a dismissal occurs. There should be no discharge, which is also known as termination. The company must find a replacement, hire, and train a new employee when a worker is fired. An ex-employee is more inclined to speak poorly of the company after being fired. When all other efforts to save the employee have failed, dismissal may be the only option.

The following are some of the factors that contribute to an employee's dismissal: Employee absenteeism, serious misconduct, false statements of qualifications, theft of business property, and other misconduct have all been cited as reasons for dismissal.

IMPLICATION OF JOB CHANGE EFFECTS OF PROMOTION

When an employee receives a promotion, they gain the authority to manage or supervise the work of others.

Employees want a promotion because of the influence it has on their income, power, responsibility, and their potential to influence broader corporate decision-making. Promotions are seen as an opportunity for advancement.

Promotions typically come with increased monetary compensation as well as the psychological boost that comes from feeling like you've accomplished something.

A promotion can be an effective means of conveying to employees what is highly appreciated at a company.

Effects of Demotion:

Employees who have been demoted have been given a clear message that their actions have been found to be in violation of company policy.

- Other colleagues who work with the degraded person may feel demoralised as a result.
- Need fulfilment will be seriously impacted by a reduction in status.

Causes of Demotion

It's possible to utilise demotion as a tool for reining in misbehaving employees.

It's possible that after being promoted, an employee will be demoted if he or she fails to meet the work requirements.

CONTROL PROCESS

Ascertain whether or not a business is succeeding in its goals. It compares performance with desired outcome and gives the feedback necessary for management to evaluate results and take remedial action, as needed.

A Five Step Feedback Model:
Determine what to measure :

Top management and operational managers need to identify what implementation process and results must be capable of being measured in a suitably objective and consistent manner.

Establish standards of performance:

Performance standards are specific representations of strategic objectives that serve as a gauge for what constitutes acceptable levels of performance. **Measure performance** The measurement must be conducted at regular periods.

Compare actual performance with the standard:

Providing real-world outcomes fall within the expected tolerances. The measurement process stops here.

Take corrective action:

To determine what action needs to be taken if actual findings fall outside of the specified tolerance range

Measuring performance

The final product of a process. Which metrics to select assess performance depends on the organisational unit to be appraised and the purpose to be reached.

GRIEVANCE

According to the dictionary, "grievance" means "any dissatisfaction that has a negative impact on organizational relations." The distinction between dissatisfaction, complaint, and grievance is crucial to comprehend what a grievance is.

There are two types of complaints: those that are made verbally or in writing, and those that are made in person.

There are three types of grievances: formal complaints, informal complaints, and informal complaints.

An expression of unhappiness, whether spoken or not, written or unwritten, justifiable or unjustified, with regard to one's employment condition is referred to as a grievance.

CAUSES OF GRIEVANCES:

1. Economic:

Individual compensation modifications may be requested by employees. They may believe that they are underpaid relative to their peers. A few examples include: unpaid bonuses, untimely payments, modifications to overtime pay, accusations of unequal treatment, calls for equal pay, and appeals against pay based on performance.

2. Work environment:

Unpleasant or unpleasant working conditions may be a contributing factor. A lack of light, heat, or space; defective tools and equipment; poor quality materials; unjust rules; and a lack of acknowledgment are examples of occupational hazards.

3. Supervision:

General techniques of supervision may be criticised for their apparent biases, favoritisms, nepotisms and caste-affiliated views of the supervisor towards the employee.

4. Organizational change:

Grievances can arise from any organizational policy change. For example, a company policy change or a new way of working.

5. Employee relations:

Inter-employee disagreements and emotions of neglect and victimisation can lead to an inability to adapt to one's coworkers, as well as a host of other problems.

6. Miscellaneous:

Issues connected to specific transgressions in terms of disciplinary rules (such as providing leaves and medical facilities), promotion techniques (such as safety measures), transfer, etc.

GRIEVANCE HANDLING PROCEDURE

Step-by-step procedure for an employee to file a grievance and have it dealt with appropriately. When an employee files a grievance with management, the process is referred to as a "grievance procedure." Organizations have varying grievance procedures.

STEPS IN GRIEVANCE HANDLING

1. Acknowledge and understand grievance

The first step in grievance handling is to appropriate recognize the problems before they turn into actual grievances through several means such as:

Observation: Managers and supervisors can simply observe the behaviour of those who work under them. He'll have no trouble spotting any odd behaviour and putting together a report about it.

Opinion surveys: Employee dissatisfaction can also be discovered through regular meetings, group discussions, and collective bargaining sessions with workers.

Gripe boxes: Complaints can be deposited in this box. There is no need for employees to reveal their identities when voicing their sense of unfairness or dissatisfaction.

Exit interviews: A common reason for employees to quit their existing occupations is that they are dissatisfied in some aspect of their work environment. When conducted correctly, exit interviews can yield valuable insight into the problems faced by employees.

Gathering facts and data

The next stage is to gather information from all parties engaged in the dispute. No one's viewpoint is more important than anyone else's, and no truth should be ignored or overlooked.

Analysis of the grievance

The problem should be assessed using the facts and data that have been collected, taking into account the economic, social, psychological, and legal aspects of the situation.

Deriving a solution

When all the facts and data have been analysed, various solutions to the problem should be considered and the best one should be chosen.

Redressed

The optimal remedy should be implemented as soon as possible to address the issue. Worker tension and unhappiness must be alleviated immediately.

Execution and Follow up

There should be a timely follow-up to document the employee's reaction once the solution is introduced and implemented. To ensure that the issue is correctly closed and that it does not recur, it should be rechecked frequently.

●

UNIT-6
INDUSTRIAL RELATIONS

INTRODUCTION

Industrial Relations, on the other hand, has a wide and a narrow definition. Labor-management ties, including those between unions and the state, as well as those between businesses and the federal government, are all included under the umbrella term "Industrial Relations." If taken strictly, it covers all kinds of interactions between employers and employees, unions and management, workplaces and labour unions, and workers themselves. It also encompasses all kinds of connections within the company, both formal and informal. IR (Internal Relations) refers to the relationships among persons working in a particular industry.

"Industrial relations are the complicated interrelations among managers, workers, and government authorities."

"Industrial relations is the process of management negotiating with one or more unions with a goal to establish and afterwards administer collective bargaining agreement or labour contract".

TRADE UNION

"A Trade Union is an organisation of employees, acting collectively, who strive to safeguard and promote their common interests through collective bargaining".

FUNCTIONS OF TRADE UNION
1. Militant Functions

All of the union's actions are aimed at enhancing the job position of its members. These responsibilities are inextricably linked to securing acceptable income or salaries, better working and employment circumstances, and access to better medical care, among other things.

2. Fraternal Functions

The next task is to assist workers in increasing their productivity by offering assistance when needed. It also develops the labour spirit and motivates amicable links between the industry and scatter education as well as a culture among the workforce.

3. Social Functions:

Apart from the economics tasks of the Trade Union such as organising unions and improving terms and conditions, the union started providing a wide array of welfare services to the workers as well as to the community.

4. Political functions:

This function is related with acquiring the affiliation from the political party an assisting them in registering more and more members, in return the political parties helping the trade union during the period of strikes and lockouts.

TYPES OF TRADE UNION

1. Classification on the basis of Ideology

1. **Revolutionary Unions**: This kind of union is linked to the belief that the social and economic system may be transformed and a new one created. This could also lead to a shift in the balance of power.

2. **Reformist or Welfare Unions**: As part of the contemporary framework of the socioeconomic and political European model, it is linked to changes in working conditions.

3. **Uplift Unions**: Beyond the domain of working conditions, it is associated with the wide reforms such as making changes in the taxation system, eliminating the poverty and so on.

2. Classification on the basis of trade

Few unions have members and jurisdictions based on the professions they represent. Workers who are qualified in certain trades or crafts, such as pipe fitting, secretarial work, carpentry, and so on, are included in the Craft Union's narrow membership. India and Sri Lanka have less of these unions, but they are more widespread elsewhere in the western world.

3. Classification on the basis of an agreement

1. **Union Shop**: It comprises a specified amount of time within which a worker must join the trade union following employment and it is a form of agreement which is known as a union shop.

2. **Preferential Shop:** It has to do with giving a member preference. Preferential Shop is a term used to describe an agreement in which employees are given more priority when filling open positions.

3. **Maintenance Shop:** In this form of shop, there is no such required membership in the union, not before and after the recruitment. The worker must, however, remain a union member for the duration of their job if they choose to join a union. A membership store is another name for this type of establishment.

PROBLEMS OF TRADE UNIONS

Small Size: Despite an increase in both the number of unions and the number of members, the average membership of most unions is insufficient to be effective.

Weak Financial Position: Union members make a pittance on a yearly basis, which is woefully inadequate. The subscription fees are modest and many users do not pay the subscription in time. Due to their financial difficulties, most of the unions are not in a position to undertake benefit schemes for workers.

Multiplicity of Unions: Several unions exist within the same company or industry. The unhealthy expansion of the Indian labour movement can be attributed in large part to the existence of competing unions with divergent ideologies. In some circumstances, companies induce division in unions to undercut their bargaining ability.

Opposition from Employers: Employers in India are a persistent obstacle for labour unions. Many businesses try to coerce or victimise labour leaders, organise rival unions and bribe union officials; thus, contradicting the fundamental aims of their formation.

Inter-Union Rivalry: Multiple labour unions lead to competition. Unions aim to play down each other in order to obtain more influence among employees. Taking advantage of a situation when employees are battling each other is common practise among employers. The power of collective bargaining is weakened and employees' ability to protect their lawful rights is reduced when there is competition among unions.

INDUSTRIAL DISPUTES

Conflicts in the workplace are organised demonstrations against the terms and circumstances of employment as they currently exist. "Any dispute or difference between employer and employer or between employer and workmen or between workmen and workmen, which is connected with the employment or non-employment or terms of employment or with the conditions of labour of any person"

Any individual's personal grievances have no place in a workplace conflict. It typically has a significant impact on a wide number of members of the labour community who share common goals and concerns.

CAUSES OF INDUSTRIAL DISPUTE
Economic Factors:

Industrial disputes are frequently sparked by issues related to compensation, incentives, benefits, and investments aimed at improving working conditions.

i. Wages:

The most common bone of disagreement between labour and management is the desire of workers to have their wages raised. This becomes the more significant issue because of the wage differentials along industrial sectors, regional levels, and geographical levels. Wage disparities are viewed as unfair by industrial workers who compare their pay with those of their peers in other industries.

Disagreements over wage differentials tend to be more frequent than those over other types of differentials. For example, the primary basis of industrial conflict which led to violence and lock-out at Lucknow factory of Tata Motors has been the demand for parity of pay prevailing in other plants of the firm.

ii. Incentives:

Besides salaries, incentives also become matter of conflict between workers and management. Incentive system becomes source of disagreements because of three reasons.

First, workers may believe that incentives are not appropriate in relation to the company's profit which is earned via their labour.

Second, even though incentives may be judged adequate, there may be controversy about the problem of linking incentives and performance.

Workers and unions may also object to the methodology used in determining incentives, which brings us to our final point. In fact, trade unions have not accepted the claim of the management that the profit of a corporation should be taken as reported in its annual reports. They dispute about the treatment of certain charges in the books of account.

iii. Benefits:

Various forms of benefits, both statutory and voluntary, are provided by organisations to their employees. Dissatisfaction among employees and disputes between labour and management are frequently caused by such elements as leave with wages, medical benefits, pensions and other fund benefits, facilities for subsidised services for employees and their dependents, among others.

iv. Working Conditions:

Conditions of employment, including physical facilities and the physical work environment, cause stress in workers when they fall short of the required criteria. Many firms do not care to offer even the mandated minimal physical amenities such as light, ventilation, safety devices, pollution control devices, and physical facilities which a normal individual requires at the job.

In fact, at several sites, the working circumstances are so terrible that these might be described as inhuman. Industrial disagreements are exacerbated by other aspects of the job, such as the hours worked, the shift system, and so on.

Management Practices:

Disagreements often arise as a result of management actions that are either illegal or discriminatory against employees. Such behaviours may be in the form of unfair labour practises, poor monitoring, and breach of acceptable norms prevailing in the business.

i. Unfair Labour Practices:

There are numerous labour practises employed by management which may lead to industrial conflicts.

ii. Ineffective Supervision:

On a daily basis, employees interact with supervisors on the front lines of their organisations. If these bosses are not successful and well-behaved, they treat the workers inhumanely by adopting the age-old master-servant relationships.

In an authoritarian workplace, workers may not feel free to express their concerns, which may indicate that things are going well in the workplace in terms of industrial relations, but the situation could quickly deteriorate and lead to a serious industrial dispute.

iii. Violation of Acceptable Norms:

Management can breach acceptable norms in reality even when those norms exist on paper in the organisation in a variety of ways. Various such regulations may be in the form of Code of Discipline, grievance procedure, agreements entered into between labour and management, discrimination in offering promotion and providing training, etc.

Trade Union Practices:

Besides the management procedures, there are several trade union practises which lead to creation of industrial disputes. Such tactics may be classified into two categories- union rivalry and non-cooperative approach.

i. Union Rivalry:

In India, there is a problem of overcrowding in the labour movement. In many companies, more than one union exists; in some cases more than four. In such a circumstance, each union professes to progress the cause of workers so as to draw them to its fold.

The effect is that any settlement reached at between management and a union is opposed by other unions irrespective of the most favourable conditions for the employees in the current situation. Such a rivalry among unions leads to violence and other such problems and the disagreements become natural outcomes.

ii. Non-Cooperative Approach:

Many trade unions and their leaders proceed on the idea that 'what they do is right and what management does is wrong'. Such a predisposition on the side of trade unions pushes them to adopt non-cooperative stance and they resist any settlements. For example,

Ramaswamy has remarked that "CITU follows a pristine model of trade unionism rooted from the notion of class conflict.

Legal and Political Factors:

Unnecessary interference in an organization's or industry's industrial relations system is caused by a variety of legal and political issues. There are two types of these factors: the proliferation of labour legislation and political meddling in the system of labour relations.

i. Multiplicity of Labour Laws:

The goal of enacting labour laws in any country is to improve working conditions for everyone. However, existence of various employment regulations produces more confusions and litigations in the pretence of their being comprehensive. In India, there are two types of challenges in this respect. To begin, there are 108 pieces of legislation and standards governing labour relations.

The underlying conflicts among these laws exist. Industrial relations departments of many corporations as well as trade unions remain busy to discover the legal loophole to leverage this in their favour.

Second, most of the labour regulations have been enacted long ago and many of them even before the independence. Constitution of India, adopted in 1950, has seen many revisions but the labour laws have remained unaltered. Even though many bills to change various statutes have been prepared, no further progress has been made.

Since the period, various labour laws have been adopted, the scenario has changed, attitudes of both workers and management have changed, and international human resource management methods have altered. In the altered context, these labour rules have outlived their utility to a very significant amount; they have become source of industrial disputes.

ii. Political Interference:

Political influence in the industrial relations system also contributes in the creation of industrial disputes. Political intervention is through the politicisation of labour union activity or outright interference of political parties and its workers.

MACHINERY FOR SETTLEMENT OF INDUSTRIAL DISPUTES:

1. Conciliation: Conciliation refers to the procedure by which representatives of employees and employers are brought together before a third party with a view to debate, reconcile their disagreements and come at an agreement by mutual consent. The third party works as a facilitator in this process. Conciliation is a sort of state intervention in settling the Industrial Disputes. The Industrial Disputes Act authorises the Central & State governments to appoint conciliation officers and a Board of Conciliation as and when the situation warrants.

2. Arbitration: Unbiased party listens to each side, gathers facts, and makes a final conclusion that is binding on both sides of the argument. The conciliator simply encourages the parties to come to a settlement, whereas the arbitrator listens to both the parties and then offers his judgement.

Arbitration Offers the Following Benefits:

• It is formed by the parties themselves and so both parties have good faith in the arbitration process. \s• The process in informal and flexible in nature. \s• It is based on mutual consent of the parties and hence aids in building Good Industrial Relations.

Disadvantages:

Arbitration can take a long time to resolve conflicts, and the costs are split between workers and management. Arbitration can also lead to arbitrary decisions if the arbitrator is unqualified or biassed.

Arbitration can be divided into two categories:

Voluntary Arbitration: In a voluntary arbitration, the arbitrator is chosen by both parties with their cooperation and only acts when the issue is referred to him by the other party or parties involved in the arbitration.

Compulsory Arbitration: This implies that the parties must submit their disagreement to the arbitrator, regardless of how they feel about him. If the parties are unable to resolve their differences amicably, or if there is some other compelling reason, the government can compel the parties to seek the services of an arbitrator.

3. Adjudication: Adjudication is the ultimate legal procedure for settlement of Industrial Dispute. Adjudication involves intervention of a legal authority appointed by the government to make a settlement which is binding on both the parties. A labour court or a panel must adjudicate an industrial issue as a matter of law in order for it to be considered adjudicated.

EMPLOYEE GRIEVANCE
CONCEPT

To be dissatisfied or unhappy with something about one's job because of something that employee perceives to be unjust. A grievance can be true, fictional or concealed.

A grievance emerges when an employee goes through an unfair, unjust or inequitable condition or treatment at the job. Over time, the employee who feels wronged builds up enough resentment to file a formal complaint.

CAUSES OF GRIEVANCE
Inadequate Wages and Bonus

When the workers are not paid an acceptable quantity of pay and bonuses for their hard work or if equal wages are not paid for the same labour, the grievance may occur.

Unachievable and Irrational Targets and Standards

Managers can set goals that are impossible to meet because they are unrealistic. Employees' dissatisfaction grows as they are put under increasing amounts of stress and pressure in the pursuit of company goals.

Bad Working Conditions

An employee's degree of happiness at work is strongly influenced by their working conditions. Bad working conditions, shortage of equipment and suitable machinery can contribute to dissatisfaction amongst the staff.

Inadequate Health and Safety Sevices

While focusing on increasing their bottom line, companies neglect the well-being of their workers in the process. Employees are less likely to show up to work if they have to deal with an unsanitary working environment, unsafe working conditions, and so on.

Strained Relationship Amongst the Employees

When working with coworkers, whether superiors or subordinates, the employee may experience feelings of resentment, jealousy, anxiety, and other negative emotions. When there is a lack of positive interactions between coworkers, an atmosphere of sadness, dissatisfaction, and resentment develops.

Layoffs and Retrenchment

Every business tries to lower the strength of its personnel during a financial collapse in order to reduce the overall cost. Ones who are laid off as a result of these situations feel tricked, and the employees who are kept on feel threatened.

GRIEVANCE REDRESSAL PROCEDURE

Acknowledging Grievance

Employees should be able to voice any concerns or grievances they have without fear of retaliation from their superiors or managers, and managers and supervisors should encourage open communication between them and their staff.

Acknowledgement of their difficulties instils confidence in them that they are in safe hands and their problems will be remedied.

Quick Action

As we all know justice delayed is justice denied. When a complaint is resolved at the earliest possible stage, it shows the employee that management cares about his or her concerns and is making an effort to address them. The grievance procedure must aim at a fast settlement of a problem.

Adherence to Prevailing Law

Redress should be planned according to current legislation. The existing legal mechanisms for redressing grievances should be scrupulously adhered to, in other words.

Clarity

The technique should be straightforward and basic enough to be comprehended by each and every employee. Every employee must thoroughly grasp the different steps of the operation, the forms to be filled up etc

Grievance Handling Training should be given to Senior

Those who guide, oversee, or spend the most time with employees at work—supervisors and union representatives—need to receive training in these areas.

When issues develop, they will be brought to their attention right away, making it much more efficient to handle them there and then rather than escalating the situation.

Execution and review (follow up)

People's faith in the system is bolstered when it is regularly monitored. The HR department should routinely assess the grievance procedure of an organisation and make the appropriate modifications whenever required.

DISCIPLINE

To achieve a controlled performance, discipline is the control and modification of human activity. Discipline has a very straightforward purpose. It's a way to motivate workers to meet specified criteria of job performance and to conduct themselves in a safe and responsible manner at work. Every well-organized group activity necessitates discipline.

Procedures for correcting or punishing a subordinate who has broken a rule of procedure are called discipline.

The following is an excerpt from a 2001 article by l Dessen:

An organization's norms, standards, and policies should be clearly communicated to its employees so that they understand the repercussions of breaking them.

MAJOR ASPECTS OF DISCIPLINE.

Negative Discipline Punishment for disobedience or indiscipline is a traditional part of discipline that is associated with making sure subordinates conform to the rules. As you can see, in this perspective, the punishments for breaking the rules are severe. Subordinates are deterred from misbehaving by the dread of punishment. For a variety of reasons, this approach of discipline has become increasingly ineffective.

Positive Discipline: The most crucial factor in positive discipline is a person's willingness to cooperate. The focus here is on the importance of working together to ensure that organizational rules are adhered to. Your subordinates' requirements and your company's goals can be met by using this disciplinary strategy. Therefore, it would inspire your employees to work hard and meet their objectives. In other words, positive discipline demands that your employees fully comprehend the goals and expected standards of behaviour in your workplace. Self-discipline is assumed to be a part of the positive concept of discipline.

Discipline as Self-control: Training that corrects, moulds, strengthens or perfects one's behaviour is discipline at one level. As a person's efforts at self-control for the goal of adapting to specific needs and demands, discipline is defined as self-discipline. This is pure self-control at its finest. You and your subordinates will agree with us that this kind of self-discipline is critical to achieve your organization's goals successfully and efficiently. The focus here is once again on developing and maintaining a basic level of organization. Increasing the degree and extent of subordinate compliance is the key to achieving this orderliness in the modern workplace.

ASPECTS OF DISCIPLINE

1. Positive Aspect

Employees follow regulations not because they're afraid of being punished, but because they want to work together to accomplish something. Where two-way communication, clear goals and good leadership characterise the corporate climate, employees need not be indiscipline in the traditional way.

Positivity, constructive discipline, and self-discipline are all terms used to describe this approach. According to Spriegel, "positive discipline helps an employee to have a greater freedom in that he enjoys a greater degree of self-expression in attempting to attain the collective purpose, which he sees as his own".

2. Negative Aspect:

Employees sometimes may not believe in and support discipline. As such, they do not conform to laws, regulations and expected level of behaviour. Punishment and other forms of punishment used in a disciplinary programme actually force and limit employees to follow directions and do their duties in line with established rules and regulations.

DISCIPLINARY PROCEDURE
1. Charge-Sheeting:

If you want to take disciplinary action against an employee, the first thing you should do is charge-sheet him, which means asking him why he should not be punished for his misconduct. The charge-sheet has to be specific and should describe the offence committed by him, the place, date and time of the offence committed. He is afforded sufficient time to respond.

You have the option of giving the employee a copy of the charge-sheet in person or sending it to him via registered mail if he refuses to accept it. The employee may be exonerated of the charge or given a minor punishment with a warning if he admits his guilt and swears not to repeat it. Providing the criminal an opportunity to defend his position is based on the idea of natural justice as enshrined under Article 311 of the Indian Constitution.

The Article reads, "No person shall be dismissed or removed from service until he has been given a reasonable opportunity to show cause why the proposed action should not be taken against him." In a landmark decision, the Supreme Court outlined the foundational elements of natural justice for the first time.

2. Domestic Enquiry/Enquiry:

In case the management is not pleased with the outcome of the charge-sheeting and deems the offence as of serious nature, it proceeds with the procedure of domestic enquiry or enquiry. At this point, management notifies the employee of the investigation, names a company officer or an impartial third party to conduct it, and notifies the relevant parties.

The investigator must conduct a thorough investigation, gather evidence and information pertinent to the case, speak with the employee and other coworkers and stakeholders, and document the events and testimony of witnesses. On the completion of the enquiry, the enquiry officer presents his report to the appointing authority. It's not uncommon for the investigation officer to recommend that a punishment be imposed on an employee if they are found guilty of the infraction.

As the enquiry is frequently handled by an officer of the establishment itself, it is dubbed a "domestic enquiry." In some circumstances, the responsibility of conducting enquiry is given to an outside neutral person or agency.

3. Inflicting Punishment:

After considering the report of the enquiry officer, statements of witnesses and other material evidences, and the recommendations of the enquiry officer as regards the type of punishment to be inflicted on him, the management takes the final decision in the matter and issues an order for implementation. A copy of the order is also served on the guilty employee.

Indiscipline and violence have comprised a large fraction of the total number of industrial conflicts in the country for the last many years. Disciplinary cases, notably those ending in dismissal, discharge or retrenchment, have given rise to a considerable number of litigations under the Industrial Disputes Act, 1947 and associated state statutes. Many such disputes have also gone before High Courts and even the highest Supreme Court for determination.

In quite a number of cases, the adjudication authorities and courts have nullified the decision of the management and awarded relief to the employees in various ways such as reinstatement, exoneration of the charge, payment of compensation and so on, many of which have been highly embarrassing and humiliating for the management.

COLLECTIVE BARGAINING
CONCEPT

"Collective Bargaining is a procedure in which the representatives of a labour organisation and the representatives of business organisation meet and attempt to negotiate a contract or agreement, which outlines the nature of employee-employer union relationship".

To fix the terms of employment, employers and unions use collective bargaining to negotiate with organised groups of employees, who are represented by authorised agents. "The essence of collective bargaining is bargaining between interested parties, not from outside parties," according to the authors.

TYPES OF COLLECTIVE BARGAINING

Conjunctive or Distributive Bargaining: In this kind of collective bargaining, both the parties viz. The employee and the employer aim to maximise their respective gains. It is based on the idea, "my gain is your loss, and your gain is my loss" i.e. one side wins over the other.

The economic issues such as wages, bonus, other perks are discussed, where the employee wishes to have an enhanced wage or bonus for his work done, whereas the employer wishes to increase the workload and lower the wages.

Co-operative or Integrative Bargaining: Both the employee and the employer meet to discuss issues of mutual concern in an effort to find a mutually beneficial solution. In the event of an unavoidable economic downturn, such as the current one, it may be possible to come to an agreement on the terms of employment.

Productivity Bargaining: This sort of negotiating is done by the management, where the workers are offered the incentives or the bonus for the higher production. Employees are motivated to go above and beyond the standard productivity level in order to reap the additional benefits.

Both the company and the employee benefit from this form of collective bargaining, which results in increased output and higher wages.

Composite Bargaining: Collective bargaining in this manner aims to preserve workers' interests and prevent the dilution of their power by addressing problems such as pay and working conditions as well as environmental concerns, mergers and amalgamations with other businesses and pricing policies.

PROCESS OF COLLECTIVE BARGAINING

Preparation: Prior to the meeting, both parties' representatives prepare their respective positions on the issues to be discussed. Each participant should be thoroughly informed with the problems to be presented at the meeting and should have enough knowledge of the labour regulations.

The management should be well prepared with the ideas of change required in the employment terms and be ready with the statistical facts to defend its viewpoint.

On the other hand, the union must gather appropriate information regarding the financial position of the firm together with its ability to pay and write a complete report on the issues and the desires of the workers.

Discuss: Negotiations begin with a set of ground rules agreed upon by all parties, and a member of the management team serves as the primary negotiator. Also, the topics for which the meeting is organised, are identified at this point.

The difficulties could be related to the pay, supplemental economic benefits (pension plans, health insurance, paid holidays, etc.), Institutional issues(rights and obligations, ESOP plan), Administrative issues (health and safety, technological advances, job security, working conditions) (health and safety, technological changes, job security, working conditions).

Propose: The main negotiator will make an opening speech, followed by a statement from each party outlining their initial demands. This session might be characterised as a brainstorming, where each party expresses their perspective that leads to arguments and counter arguments.

Bargain: The negotiation begins at this point, as one party seeks to win over the other. The negotiation can proceed for days until a final deal is achieved. Sometimes an agreeable settlement is reached quickly by both sides, but sometimes a third party enters the negotiation in the form of arbitration or adjudication to decide the disagreement.

Settlement: This is the final step of the collective bargaining process, where both the parties agree on a shared solution to the problem discussed so far. A written agreement between the employee and the employer is therefore drafted, and each party must sign it before the decision may be considered final.

Thus, to get the issue settled the management must follow these processes consistently and give equal chance to the workers to voice out their opinions.

ESSENTIALS OF EFFECTIVE COLLECTIVE BARGAINING.
1. Favorable Political and Social Climate:

The history of collective bargaining around the world confirms the need of a favourable political and social atmosphere for successful negotiations. In countries where it has had official support and public support, collective bargaining has made progress in resolving industrial disputes. Therefore, India's political environment does not favour collective bargaining.

The reason is not far to seek. A wide variety of political parties have sponsored trade unions around the country. Rather than taking sides based on what is best for workers, many unions favour their members based on ideological differences. Added to these is a multiplicity of legislative restrictions thus generating unfriendly climate for collective bargaining in the country.

2. Trade Unions:

Like in a democratic country like ours, employees should have fundamental rights to organise trade unions for preserving their interests. More the stronger the trade union f lay successful collective bargaining and vice versa. The employer should also recognise a trade union and its representatives.

3. Problem Solving Attitude:

Both the sides during negotiating should have a problem solving, or say compromise mindset to reach an agreement. The uncompromising or combative aide should be avoided by both parties. In negotiations, a give-and-take strategy is recommended. It suggests that one party may obtain concessions over the other depending upon their relative powers.

4. Availability of Data:

Data and information serve as inputs for decision-making. Hence, the availability of essential data serves as a pre-requisite tor successful collective bargaining. While the employer Ike available data essential for collective discussion, their union representatives also must accept and trust on data offered by the company.

5. Continuous Dialogue:

Collective bargaining sometimes may not arrive to an agreement. In- stead, there may be standstill, or say negotiation impasse. A problem-solving technique must be used even if the discourse has come to an end. Disagreements can be narrowed and the conversation can continue if the contentious points are temporarily set aside. Possibility for agreement may improve with continuation of conversation.

●

REFERENCES

1. Human Resource Management By Sunaina Sardana.
2. Personnel and Human Resource Management Book by P. Subba Rao
3. A Textbook of Human Resource Management Textbook by C. B. Mamoria
4. Human Resources Management: Text and Cases Book by Rao V S P
5. Human Resource Management by Ashok Khurana (Author), Praveen Khurana (Author), Hira Lal Sharma (Author)
6. Managing Human Resources by J P Mahajan

www.ingramcontent.com/pod-product-compliance
Lightning Source LLC
Chambersburg PA
CBHW071210130726
47998CB00002B/695